THE WAYS OF RAIN–
MANERAS DE LLOVER

AND OTHER POEMS

by Hugo Lindo

INTRODUCTION AND TRANSLATION

BY

ELIZABETH GAMBLE MILLER

Foreword
Rainer Schulte

Editor
Yvette E. Miller

LATIN AMERICAN LITERARY REVIEW PRESS
SERIES: DISCOVERIES
PITTSBURGH, PENNSYLVANIA
1986

The Latin American Literary Review Press publishes Latin American creative writing under the series title *Discoveries* and critical works under the series title *Explorations*.

This volume has been published with funding from Dedman College of Southern Methodist University and a gift from Jane Holland Browning.

Library of Congress Cataloging-in-Publication Data
Lindo, Hugo, 1917-1985
      The ways of rain = Maneras de llover; and other selections from the poetry of Hugo Lindo
(Discoveries)
      Text in English and Spanish.
      Bibliography: p. 157.
      1. Lindo, Hugo, 1917-1985   --Translations, English.
I. Miller, Elizabeth Gamble, 1926-   . II. Lindo, Hugo, 1917-1985, Maneras de llover. English & Spanish. 1986. III. Title. IV. Series.
PQ 7539.L5A25   1986   861   86-18577
ISBN   0-935480-24-2

Some of the poems included have appeared in the following journals and anthologies, to whose editors I offer grateful acknowledgment:
Cantos from *Maneras de llover*: *Latin American Literary Review*, vol. XIV, no. 28 (July-Dec., 1986); *Mundus Artium, a Journal of International Literature and the Arts*, vol. XIV, no. 2 (1984).
Cantos from *Sólo la voz: Hugo Lindo*, *Sólo la voz/ Only the Voice*, Introduction and Translation, Elizabeth Gamble Miller, Mundus Artium Press, 1984; *New Orleans Review*, vol. 7, no. 3 (Loyola Univ., New Orleans, 1980); *New Orleans Review* , vol. XIII, no. 2 (Loyola Univ., New Orleans, 1986).   Poem from *Sinfonía del límite*: "On Poetry," *New Orleans Review*, vol. X, no. 9 (Loyola Univ., New Orleans, Winter, 1983). Reprint in *Anthology of Magazine Verse Yearbook of American Poetry* (1985). Poem from "Casi en la luz": "Between Words," *Mundus Artium; A Journal of International Literature and the Arts*, vol. XIV, no. 111 (1983).
The frontispiece was painted for this volume by Roberto Galicia.

The Spanish text was originally published as *Maneras de llover* (Madrid: Instituto de Cultura Hispánica, 1969); reprint ed., San Salvador, El Salvador: Ministerio de Educación, 1982.   Permission has been granted by Hugo Lindo, author and owner of the copyright.

The Ways of Rain/ Maneras de llover can be ordered directly from the publisher: Latin American Literary Review Press
            P.O. Box 8385
            Pittsburgh, Pennsylvania 15218

Foreword

To the last day of his life Hugo Lindo passionately tried to penetrate the shapes of words to extract from them answers that might illuminate the mystery of life. Whatever insights he drew from the depth of his own silence, he knew that he had to mold them into the possibilities of the word. And in this endeavor he rediscovered the word as image, the word as sound, and the word as rhythm. Like the master organ player he pulled all the registers to make his poetic instrument create a wholeness in a world that was losing its center. He felt the anxiety that lurked under his own and his fellow men's faces, an anxiety that was closing the avenues to human communication. He had experienced the limitations of the word and he preferred to talk about the dialogues of sounds and shadows, and he admonished us not to define what may be conveyed in hieroglyphics. It is not the function of the poet to name things when he can evoke their shadows and aromas to lead himself and the reader deeper into the realms of silence whose rivers nourish our desire and power to live and create.

Almost afraid to confront the tremendous anxiety that lurks behind the surfaces of this world, Hugo Lindo orchestrated a poetic universe where sounds, rhythms and images talk to each other. His poetry creates a softness that temporarily lets us forget the pain and suffering of this world. There are, however, a few moments in his poetry when Lindo, the seer, surprises himself with his own insights into the darker forces of human existence. Whether he ultimately thought that the human mystery could be uncovered through the power of words remains an unanswered question for Hugo Lindo. As a poet he knew that he would never free himself from living between words.

Rainer Schulte
University of Texas at Dallas

DEDICATION

Quiero dedicar la edición de este libro a la viuda de
Hugo Lindo, doña Carmen,
cuyo corazón y amor son la sustancia de su poesía

This edition is dedicated to the widow of
Hugo Lindo, doña Carmen,
whose devotion and love became his poetry

Acknowledgments

The translator is indebted to many for counsel and assistance. Special appreciation is expressed to Rainer Schulte, Sonya Ingwersen, Margaret Sayers Peden, Thomas Hoeksema and to my colleagues of the Spanish faculty of SMU, Gene Forrest, Josefina Barrera de García, John LaPrade, Conchita Winn, Samuel Zimmerman and to the Chairman of Foreign Languages, Philip Solomon.

Publications of this nature require subventions and I thank Latin American Literary Review Press, Editor Yvette Miller; Dedman College of Southern Methodist University, Dean Hal Williams; and a friend to poetry and cultural interchange, Jane Holland Browning.

I am grateful to David Escobar Galindo, Vice-Director of the Academia Salvadoreña de la Lengua, and Academic Provost of the Universidad José Matías Delgado for his support of my endeavors to bring Salvadoran literature to the English reading public.

I also wish to express my appreciation to Roberto Galicia for the frontispiece painting in honor of Hugo Lindo.

CONTENTS

"Prólogo a la noche" / Prologue to Night

"Casi en la luz" / Almost in the Light

The Ways of Rain

The Ways of Rain is Hugo Lindo's song of praise to the human race. This long lyric poem is a symbolic chant to his homeland and its patrimony, a poem of exaltation of the Central American tropics and of the "dark-haired race." In this serial madrigal the poet evokes the varying landscape of El Salvador. He juxtaposes dynamic images and strong rhythms that focus on its violent nature, "where torrents and uprootings have strength of granite," with others of gentle movement and softness, as in "waters of lament over warm ferns." Although this lyric poem of twenty-eight cantos is a chant to Central America and is inspired in the Quiché Maya creation legends in the *Popol Vuh,* it is neither topical, historical, nor, according to Hugo Lindo, is it anthropological. Through the development of the theme in which the reader becomes part of the editorial "we," *The Ways of Rain* escapes its regional and temporal frame to become a song to the tenacity of all mankind in its struggle for survival.

In this poem, as in the Mayan cosmogony revealed in the *Popol Vuh,* rain is the primordial element: water gives birth and then nurtures the life experience. Existence is perceived in a circular time frame, an eternal cycle of creation, death, and renewal: in the beginning Death observes the waters of creation, and after our own birth "we are shaped by the vertical waters of the centuries," then are comforted in death as "the ineffable water of the winter filters quietly, until it moistens the eyelids and the frozen smile."

The copious rains in El Salvador are in the winter, the summertime in Mexico and the United States, so "winter" in Lindo's poem is equated with water, the dominant metaphor in the poem. In this volume Hugo Lindo has divided the cycle of existence into seven stages, "seven winters," with rain as the protagonist. Its roles are many, its character variable: as waters of creation, lament, plenitude, sacrifice, joy, and as comforting waters, a source of resurrection. The book is, therefore, appropriately titled "The Ways of Rain."

The music of the language and vitality of the imagery are such that the poem may be enjoyed without understanding the allusions, but clarification will, perhaps, add to the pleasure. Drawn directly from the *Popol Vuh* are metaphorical references to water as the primordial element; to man made of clay, then of corn; to the plumed serpent, the Aztecs' Quetzalcoatl, giver of corn, substance of man, staple of life; to Cucumatz, the Quiché Maya counterpart of Quetzalcoatl, god/king of the seas, a fabulous being who "seven days would go to heaven and seven days would go to hell and seven days would change into a serpent,...an eagle,...a tiger..."[1]; to the *nahual*, a guardian animal given to a newborn and symbolic of his disposition; to Hunapúh and other ancestors of miraculous powers; and to the Grandparents, the bearers of the race, the original source that is also identified with water.

Directly related to the general Indian heritage of Central America are references to the *teocalli* (the Indian temple); the *copal* (incense); the *hüipil* (a loose fitting lady's garment, usually with lace or embroidery); the *huacal* and *jícara* (gourd vessels); the *chicha* (a bitter fermented drink of corn, pineapple and other ingredients); the *quetzal* (a tropical bird of symbolic brilliance, the plumed portion of *Quetzalcoatl*, the plumed serpent); the *izote* (the yucca cactus, important to the poem for its topknot of white blooms); the volcanos Izalco, Momotombo and Irazú; the *cenzontle* and other birds and animals; *tzolkín*, a time frame on the sacred calendar. The context of the poem makes the import of these terms generally clear; where appropriate, I have used them in combination with a word that will clarify meaning, such as jícara-cup, or izote-yucca, although Hugo Lindo did not clarify these for his South American or peninsular Spanish readers.

The poem begins with three introductory cantos. These build in intensity from a low-keyed conversational opening: "Let us open the book of tropical winter," as the poet evokes childhood memories with nostalgia and contrasts the bleak storybook winter of reindeer to the actual surroundings where "waters of lament" pour over sun-warmed ferns. In the second canto the tranquil tone becomes sharp and the pace quickens as the poet considers the turbulent, savage fury that is characteristic of nature in the tropics. The rhythm is slow and the tone somewhat psalmodic in the seven-lined third and final canto in which the mythic creation of Central America is proclaimed as taking place in seven winters. (Seven is a mystical number in the *Popol Vuh* as it is in the Biblical accounts of creation.) In the body of the poem these winters are revealed to be "Winter of the Rock," "Winter of Green," "...Nahual," "...Man," "...the Race," "...Death," and "Winter of the Gods."

---

[1]*Popol Vuh, Las historias del origen de los indios* (San Salvador: Ministerio de Educación, 3rd ed., 1977), pages 78 and 79, translation E.G.M. A new translation into English is available: *Popol Vuh, the Definitive Edition of the Mayan Book of the Dawn of Life and the Glories of Gods and Kings*, translated by Dennis Tedlock with commentary based on the ancient knowledge of the modern Quiché Maya, Simon and Schuster: New York (1985).

10

Water and wind and "pure, pristine pain" are the birthing forces in "Winter of the Rock." All creation is water, with Central America shown in a reverse, negative image: "a river of land hurling itself down between the two continents of raging water." Water is characterized as "powerful music" "sculpting crags." The last canto of this first section leads into "Winter of Green" by way of a vivid description of the creative action of the water:

As if the greater god,
the one of the lightning bolt,
the one of the four courses of history,
had made fertile in the flood
the virgin entrails of the earth.

In "Winter of Green" we see fertility's paradoxical nature as it moves "from primitive sterile innocence to sweet roundness of fruit." Through veiled, sensual imagery the poet evokes the birth of green: "The grey crust of the seed whimpers/ when violated by the stalk with its erect light." The identification with corn as the life-giving force is basic to Maya tradition. In the final canto of "Winter of Green" the birth of corn brings "hearth and bed, zest and life—from the waters of winter." The flora and fauna of the luxuriant tropics come into full being in "Winter of the Nahual." Oneness of man with all of nature, a theme affirmed in "Winter of the Rock"—"The rock was I myself"—is resumed as man identifies with the guardian animal, the nahual: "We are the beast in his den."

The distance between poet and reader is reduced in "Winter of Man" as Hugo Lindo, using verbs of action, dramatizes the actual amazement of Man as he makes his appearance on earth. Newly arrived, he views the active nature of creation: how "the gods were renewing the world dream by dream and the earth's womb increased in the season until the miracle." With penetrating, clear, child-like eyes he perceives the miracle: "...because the soft wells of his candor reached the shores of other worlds." Through suffering he experiences life: "...through crying from the blood itself." When the author then realizes: "I am this consciousness," we may also see ourselves in the original setting, reaping the heritage bequeathed by the animals, now acutely aware, questioning in vain the meaning of it all: "...knowing ourselves to be helpless gods ... raining our rain of endless fatigue." From this mood of deep gloom the poet moves to one of determined gratitude and even exuberance over the "ascent from the waters' infinite womb," to the time when "journey opens its rare flower." What follows is the poet's chant to woman: "...ember of unbounded tenderness... All history lies within your thighs."

The formation of the race naturally follows the encounter with woman. "Winter of the Race" evokes man's tragic conflicts and repeated oppressions, his helpless confusion in facing the present and also an unknown future, his sense of futility in regard to prayer and his feeling of guilt because of his own ingratitude. These feelings paradoxically lead him to appreciate the dormant power of man's heritage and to assert that "we with the gods will lift the race again in the world." The affirmative stance continues in "Winter of Death" where the poet views life as a continuing phenomenon, "the generations that gradually fall, drop upon drop, over the dry land," while in death the poet does not feel defeat but rather solace and a welcome refuge in the damp earth. Self-identity with all men through all time precedes the poet's affirmation of a future of centuries of death and rebirth in which "the dark-haired race," "la raza morena," will finally possess the secret of the quetzal bird and that of the plumed serpent: freedom and virtue.

In its style, "Winter of the Gods" is typical of the vigor and brilliance of the poem's imagery in general: "Drop by drop the stars force their yellow fires to fall." This final "winter" of the poem is often fanciful in tone: "they are small, irresponsible gods, that play at winter, scattering lights"; yet the intent is serious in its questioning of man's ability to speak the language of the gods and to capture their magic. In the poet's prophecy, man and his mate will always "fight the perfect battle of the children....biting the pulp of love," and traditions will continue as "together, we will ascend the steps of the temple, burning pom, asking the nahuals for the coal of the chili pepper ....for the fields' open smile." *The Ways of Rain* concludes with Rain, moving in full circle, overseeing creation, conversing with the gods, forever repeating its role of carving out man's frieze, moving "like a liquid serpent, writhing, swelling, submerging, coiling, along the endless pathways of history."

THE WAYS OF RAIN

MANERAS DE LLOVER

by

Hugo Lindo

TRANSLATOR

ELIZABETH GAMBLE MILLER

Cantos liminares

Abramos hoy el libro del invierno del trópico.
Miremos sus estampas.
¡Qué diferentes son de las del otro invierno,
del que nos referían en la alcoba del niño!

Este no tiene blancos, sino verdes,
apretados, profusos,
como saltando verde sobre verde y verde
hasta una plenitud de selva en celo.

Aquí no están presentes
el horizonte frío
ni el cielo de pizarra,
ni la luz demorosa, frágil y entumecida.

Aquí no están presentes
la elástica figura de animárbol del reno,
ni el pino con su cofia,
ni el abeto que estira largamente los brazos
conjurando al demonio cristalino del hielo.

¡Pero cuánta poesía palpitante!
¡Cuánta fuerza viril,
cuántos dioses despiertos en el rayo,
o vueltos hacia el llanto en los tibios helechos,
o reclinados dulcemente junto al musgo!

Introductory Cantos

Let us open the book of tropical winter
and let us look at its pictures!
How different they are from the other winter
as described to us in the child's bedroom!

For this one has no whites, only greens,
massed in profusion, tightly pressed,
as if green were mounted on green upon green
to the fullness of a jungle in heat.

Here there is
no cold horizon,
nor slate-colored sky
no vacillating, fragil, torpid light.

Here there is
no elastic profile of reindeer's branches,
nor topknot of pines,
no fir that stretches out its arms
conjuring the crystal devil of ice.

But what stirring poetry!
What virile strength,
how many gods astir in lightning flash,
pouring waters of lament over warm ferns,
or gently reclining beside soft moss!

Digo la selva de mi trópico
y sus marimbas verticales
anticipadas en el canto
sereno y hondo de los árboles.

Digo la luz de sus montañas,
los verdes puros y vitales
que estremecidos de potencia
hacen varón nuestro paisaje.

Digo el furor de las gargantas
en que aluviones y descuajes
tienen la fuerza del granito
y una vehemencia de catástrofe.

Digo el coyote y su aullido,
la protección de los nahuales,
el verde rayo de la iguana
bajo las yerbas palpitantes.

El lomo terso de los ríos
que van reptando entre maizales,
el vuelo sabio de las águilas
y el lento azul de su donaire.

Digo el desorden primigenio,
la hoguera viva en donde arden
las increíbles salamandras
de los poderes germinales.

Digo el invierno sin clemencia,
la furia múltiple y salvaje
con cuya mano se suaviza
el rostro nítido del aire.

Digo mi América de Enmedio:
la que comienza en las Pirámides.

I speak of the jungle of my tropics
and its vertical marimbas
with its prelude, the serene, deep
song of the trees.

I speak of the light of its mountains,
the pure, vital greens
vibrant with the potency
to make our landscape virile.

I speak of the furor of gorges
where torrents and uprootings
have strength of granite
and vehemence of catastrophe.

I speak of the coyote and its howl,
the guardian animal, the nahual,
the green stripe of the iguana
beneath pulsing grasses.

The sleek back of rivers
that are winding through corn fields,
the wise flight of eagles
and slow blue of their elegance.

I speak of the primeval disorder
the fiery holocaust wherein burn
the incredible salamanders
of generative powers.

I speak of the relentless winter,
the savage, multiple fury
in whose strokes is softened
the air's transparent face.

I speak of my Middle America:
the one that begins at the Pyramids.

17

"Los inviernos son siete" —reza el Libro.

Como los siete días que nos sacaron de la muerte
antes que el vuelo de las estaciones
comenzara quebrando las almendras
y haciendo de ellas tallos, troncos,
frutos
llenos de almendras nuevas.

"The winters are seven"—prays the Book.

Like the seven days that snatched us from death
before the seasons' flight
began splitting the almonds open
forming stalks and trunks
fruits
filled with new almonds.

Invierno de la roca

Era el día infinito
en que la muerte, echada sobre arenas parduscas,
esperaba
junto al umbral de piedra,
el nacimiento de la esponja y el tallo,
la amanecida cálida del musgo
en la matriz de alguna gruta,
el primer balbuceo de las yerbas,
la insinuación del mástil en el posible mar de la montaña.

Y solamente el agua, el agua, el viento
que azotaba sus cuerdas transparentes,
Y solamente el viento, el viento, el agua
que tejía su fibra cristalina.

Lo demás, una ausencia.

Una espantosa ausencia. Un grito
sin cauce ni garganta.
Un dolor puro,
terriblemente puro:
silencio, soledad, quietud y sombra y nada.

Winter of the Rock

It was the infinite day,
wherein death lay bedded down on dusky sands,
by the threshold of stone,
awaiting
the birth of sponge and stalk,
the warm awakening of the moss
within a cavern matrix,
the initial babble of the grasses,
the hint of mast above possible mountain sea.

And only the water, the water, the wind
whipping its transparent cords.
And only the wind, the wind, the water
weaving its cristal fibre.

The rest, an absence.

A frightening absence. A scream
without a channel or throat.
A pure, pristine
pain:
silence, solitude, calmness and shadow, and nothing.

Primero fue el invierno de las rocas,
hechas de terquedad y de silencio.
¡Mirad, mirad esta primera estampa
con todo el poderío de la memoria antigua!

¡Abrid los ojos del recuerdo
que yace más adentro del recuerdo,
y recordad!

La roca era yo mismo.
Yo. Nadie. Sin aliento ni pulso ni estupor ni tortura.
Yo, plantada en la tierra
para empezar a germinar en cien millones de años.

Yo, sin amor.
Sin voz.
Yo, duramente.

Ya desde entonces era el invierno del trópico.

Música poderosa.

El cielo derrumbado,
rajado por innumerables cuchillos de luz y cobre y fuego.

La insistencia del agua
que hiere y hiere y hiere sin descanso
y se alza y cae y cae y cae y se alza
días y días y más días,
monótona,
infatigable y escultora,
modificando aristas con su mano suavísima.

¡Ah, del basalto impuro,
de la soberbia rígida,
de nuestra impenetrable coraza de planeta!

El viento grande
coronaba los reinos de la altura
y agitaba legiones de agua inmensa
contra nuestras estatuas.

First was the winter of the rocks,
rocks of stubbornness and silence.

Look! Look at this first picture
with all the power of ancient memory!

Open your eyes to the remembrance
that lies deep within remembrance
and remember!

The rock was I, myself.
I. No one. Without breath or pulse or stupor or torture.
I, planted on earth
to begin to germinate in a hundred million years.

I, without love.
Without a voice.
I, hardbound.

Now, since that moment, was the winter of the tropics.

Powerful music.

The heavens hurled down and split open
by countless knives of light and copper and fire.

The insistence of the water
that wounds and wounds and wounds incessantly
and rises and falls and falls and falls and rises
days and days and more days
monotonously,
tirelessly
sculpting crags with its gentlest stroke.

Oh, the impure basalt,
the rigid arrogance
of our piece of impenetrable planet shell!

The great wind
crowned the kingdoms of the heights
stirred the legions of immense waters
against our statues.

Y eran nuestras estatuas insensibles
al horror, al milagro,
al fértil caos
que anticipaba informes geologías
y en las líneas ocultas del cristal, dibujaba
las futuras pirámides
por las que un ser—Yo mismo—aún no llegado,
ascendería al sol
para besar la planta de los dioses.

And insensible were our statues
to the horror, the miracle,
the fertile chaos
that came before formless geologies,
that with occult lines of crystal was designing
pyramids of the future
by which a being—I myself—still to arrive,
would ascend to the sun
to kiss the feet of the gods.

De agua son las pupilas del zafiro,
femenino, callado, subterráneo.

De agua la verde claridad del jade,
semilla de los bosques.

De agua también la noche y sus espejos
en el cuchillo de obsidiana.

Como si el dios mayor,
el del relámpago,
el de los cuatro rumbos de la historia,
hubiera fecundado en el diluvio
la entraña virgen de la tierra.

Of water, pupils of the sapphire,
feminine, hushed, subterranean.

Of water, green luster of the jade,
seed of the forests.

Of water also are the night and its mirrors
in the knife of obsidian.

As if the greater god,
the one of the lightning bolt,
the one of the four courses of history,
had made fertile in the flood
the virgin entrails of the earth.

Y la Patria cayó desde el invierno
incubada en la luz
amamantada en los pezones ásperos
del Momotombo, el Irazú, el Izalco,
llena de fuerza,
y núbil corza de ternura,
ojos de grandes lagos,
cabellera de pinos que despeina
la enarbolada música del viento.

Cayó como una grácil geografía
la cintura del mundo,
el lazo fino,
casi un río de tierra despeñándose
entre dos continentes de aguas bravas.

And the Homeland dropped from winter
incubated in light
suckled at abrasive nipples
of the Momotombo, the Irazú, the Izalco,
abounding with strength,
yet a supple doe of tenderness,
its eyes, great lakes,
its hair of pines, tousled
by the high-flown music of the wind.

It dropped as a graceful geography,
the waist of the world,
the delicate link,
almost a river of land hurling itself down
between two continents of raging waters.

Invierno del verde

He aquí la sustancia del mito verdadero:

En la entraña de piedra
nació un color.
Su nombre fue esmeralda.
Y tuvo el hambre de la luz.
Y se asomó a la superficie.
Y vio y sufrió.

Los dioses comprendieron.

"Hágase, pues, el verde sobre el páramo.
Sea el verde viviente
con mil formas,
y en él repose uno de nuestros siete rayos
para alumbrar el cinturón del mundo".

Y el verde fue.

Y él aprendió la ciencia de ir creciendo
desde el bien hasta el mal,
desde las primitivas inocencias estériles,
hasta la dulce redondez del fruto.

Winter of Green

Here we have the substance of true myth:

In the entrails of stone
was born a color.
Emerald was its name.
It hungered for light.
It sought the surface.
It saw and it suffered.

And the gods understood.

"Let there be green upon the barren plain.
Let green come alive
in a thousand forms, and resting upon it
let one of our seven rays
illumine the waist of the world."

And there was green.

And it learned the science of gradually growing
from good to evil,
from primitive sterile innocence
to sweet roundness of fruit.

En el recodo de las estaciones
la tierra duerme.

Todo su impulso germinal, discurre
debajo de la piel,
como un milagro contenido,
como un dios amarrado a la tiniebla.

El sol canta colores
en el anillo de la luz.
Cruje el terrón.
Arde la herida de la grieta.
Se alza un vaho invisible de poderosos fuegos,
y el aire duro, quema.

Pero el día en que bajan los dedos de la lluvia
y hurgan la costra seca,
todo el silencio hundido del trópico, se agita,
y el deslumbrante jade,
corazón de la selva,
comienza a palpitar con una fiebre
insólita,
increíble,
turbulenta.

Gime la costra gris de la semilla
que el tallo viola con su luz enhiesta.

Lo verde arranca de la muerte
y agita contra el día,
contra el viento,
contra el verano herido, su bandera.

En una sola noche de rumores
el trópico despierta.

La humedad es un brote innumerable.
Se torna aroma dulce.
Viste la desnudez de los ramajes,
tiende la alfombra de la hierbabuena,
y el mundo, pardo ayer,
hosco y dolido,
hace del verde fiel su santo y seña.

In the recess of the seasons
the earth slumbers.

All its procreant impetus ponders
beneath the skin,
like a miracle restrained,
like a god shackled to darkness.

The sun sings colors
within the ring of light.
The earthen clod crunches.
The wound in the fissure burns.
An invisible vapor rises from powerful fires
and the harsh air inflames.

But the day the fingers of the rain descend
and they pick at the dried crust,
all the subdued silence of the tropics stirs,
and the bedazzling jade,
the jungle's heart,
starts pulsing as from an unbelievable
strange
raging
fever.

The grey crust of the seed whimpers
when violated by the stalk with its erect light.

The green tears itself away from death
and against day,
against wind,
against wounded summer, its banner unfurls.

In a single night of murmurs
the tropics awaken.

The moistness is an infinite budding
that turns into sweet aroma
and dresses the bareness of branches;
it spreads its carpet of mint,
and the world, yesterday
brown and suffering and surly,
makes of the faithful green its saint and sign.

Si decimos maíz,
si cantamos su espada de alimento,
si hablamos de su flor
situada entre la espuma y el crepúsculo,
si enumeramos sabiamente el grano
dispuesto como ejército en batalla,
pronunciamos su estuche, largo y tibio,
su dulce estuche de barbadas felpas,
si rezamos su harina,
silenciosa
como las vírgenes de los sacrificios...

Si decimos maíz,
y recordamos cómo la cosecha
trajo el amor e iluminó los ranchos,
y cómo la sequía fue alarido
de la milpa y del hambre al mismo tiempo.
Si la memoria puede relatarnos
uno por uno su aluvión de dones,
su morosa estatura en el verano
y su genuflexión ante los vientos.
Si la lengua,
bendita en sus sabores,
va a pronunciar su espíritu y su fécula,
y a decir del fogón,
cuando lo enciende
la sonrisa candeal de las mazorcas.
Si repetimos la aventura lenta
que comenzó en un surco de los cielos,
se quedó palpitando
en las solemnes manos de los dioses,
y descendió a la tierra
para empezar las formas de la raza...

Si decimos maíz...

Y el viento sabe
acariciar sus plumas con deleite,
reconstruir los acentos del origen,
alzar canciones de abundancia y júbilo,
repetir al oído de los hombres
la sustancia inicial, de pan mostrenco,
cuando el maíz levanta su promesa
—hogar y lecho y entusiasmo y vida—
desde las aguas del invierno.

If we speak of corn,
if we sing of its nourishing blade,
if we talk of its flower
that blooms between foam and dusk,
if we wisely enumerate the grain
in readiness like an army for battle,
pronounce its husks, tepid and long,
its sweet husks with bearded hair,
if we pray of its flour,
silent,
like sacrificial virgins...

If we speak of corn
and remember how its harvest
brought love and lighted huts,
and how drouth was at once a cry
of the cornfield and of hunger.
If remembrance can recount to us
one by one its flood of gifts,
its dilatory stature in summer
and its genuflection before the winds.
If the tongue,
blessed in its flavors,
will pronounce its spirit and its starch,
and speak of the hearth
when illumined
by the wheat smile of the tassels.
If we repeat the slow adventure
that began in heavens' furrows,
and continued to pulse
in the solemn hands of the gods,
and descended to earth
to begin the forms of the race...

If we speak of corn...

And the wind knows the way
to caress its plumes with delight,
to entone again the accents of origin,
to raise up songs of abundance and joy,
to repeat for the ear of man
the initial substance, made of coarse bread,
when the corn lifts up its promise
—hearth and bed, zest and life—
from the waters of winter.

Invierno del nahual

Y nacieron la espora, el alga suave,
el cuchillo de plata
que corta las entrañas del océano.

Y fueron separadas por la mano del trueno
las aguas verticales
y el llanto echado sobre el haz del mundo.

Y cada bestia tuvo un nombre mágico
para decir su inútil inocencia.

Aguila se llamó el furor con alas.
Mariposa, la luz.
Serpiente el mal, con su sabiduría.
Cenzontle el canto amaneciendo al aire.
Tortuga, la quietud casi de piedra,
casi de eternidad, casi de muerte,
y Paloma el amor.

Y Afán mi nombre.

Winter of the Nahual

And there were born the spore, the soft algae,
the knife of silver
that slices the entrails of the ocean.

And separated by thunder's hand
were the vertical waters
and those of the lament over the surface of the earth.

And each beast had a magic name
to say its useless innocence.

Eagle was the name of winged furor.
Butterfly, the light.
Serpent, evil, with its wisdom.
Cenzontle, mocking song awakening the air.
Turtle, the almost stonelike stillness,
almost like eternity, almost like death,
and Dove, the name of love.

And Zeal, my name.

Aquí brinca el cusuco,
piedra móvil
que surge de la boca de la mina.

Aquí el cenzontle canta,
trino de suave pluma
recién cuajado en la mitad del aire.

Aquí un hervor de insectos
araña con sus ruidos
la verde realidad del monte bárbaro.

Aquí el bífido tallo
de Quetzalcoatl, vestido de colores,
custodia la montaña y el bejuco.

Aquí el venado elástico,
estampa de la fuga,
relámpago de ramas azoradas.

Aquí la iguana fría,
yerba veloz entre las yerbas quietas,
raudo hilván de marañas y escondites.

Aquí el súbito puma,
sigiloso oficiante del peligro,
semidiós del pavor y de la muerte.

Aquí el coyote, diente de la noche,
aullido con punta de obsidiana,
pelaje gris del miedo y la ignominia.

Y la lluvia, bajando sus cortinajes de agua,
obligando el amor de la guarida,
juntando cuerpos,
revolviendo instintos,
hinchando las matrices de la selva,
tutelando el milagro silencioso
de la perpetuidad en la ardentía.

Here the armadillo frolics,
a mobile stone
emerging from the mouth of the mine.

Here the cenzontle is singing
a trill of its gentle plumage
recently congealed in the middle of the air.

Here the seething of the insects
noisily scratches
the green reality of savage wilderness.

Here the bifid stalk
of Quetzalcoatl, clothed in colors,
watches over mountain and reed.

Here the elastic deer,
image of flight,
lightning bolt of flustered branches.

Here the cold iguana,
swift grass among the quiet grasses,
quickly stitches through thickets and hiding places.

Here the sudden puma,
stealthy priest of danger,
demigod of dread and death.

Here the coyote, tooth of the night,
the howl with obsidian point,
grey pelt of fear and ignominy.

And the rain, lowering its curtains of water,
forcing love within the den,
uniting bodies,
stirring instincts,
swelling matrixes of the jungle,
tutoring the silent miracle
of the faithfulness of ardor.

Nahual,
signo del hombre,
marca de su fervor y su destino,
guía del vuelo y de la fuerza,
de la crueldad y la canción.

Nahual,
dios escondido,
nombre secreto,
mágica sustancia,
sello del cielo en nuestra carne, rumbo,
última realidad de nuestro aliento.

Somos la bestia en su guarida.

La soledad del águila en la más alta patria,
donde el rayo y el trueno
edifican sus templos de tormenta.

La aguja de colores
que pespunta de asombro la selva de quetzales
donde la luz se vuelve pájaro.

La garra carnicera,
el ojo listo
y el más templado impulso de la musculatura.

El canto amaneciendo
en la garganta fluida del cenzontle.

La sabia sordidez
que acecha entre las hojas enroscada.

La quietud,
casi de ídolo,
con que el ojo tenaz del tecolote perfora las tinieblas.

O el brillo verde azul,
semilla intermitente de fogata,
que trae la luciérnaga
desde el lejano mundo de los astros.

Nahual,
sign of man,
mark of his fervor and his fate,
guide for flight and force,
for cruelty and song.

Nahual,
hidden god,
secret name,
magic substance,
seal of heaven in our flesh, our course,
ultimate reality of our breath.

We are the beast in his den.

The solitude of the eagle in the loftiest homeland,
where lightning ray and thunder
construct their temples of storm.

The needle of colors
that stitches the quetzals' jungle in needlepoint of amazement
where light becomes bird.

The carnivorous talon,
the alert eye
and the most tempered impulse of the muscles.

The song awakening
in the liquid throat of the mockingbird.

The wise sordidness
that lies in wait while coiled among the leaves.

The stillness,
almost that of an idol,
with which the owl's persistent eye pierces darkness.

Or the sparkle of blue-green,
the hearth's flickering seed
that the firefly brings
from the distant world of the stars.

Invierno del hombre

Primero, en los ardores agrios de la sequía,
las pupilas del hombre
quemaban las imágenes
inventando fantasmas de ceniza,
estériles jardines,
rosas de cal,
guirnaldas de hojarasca.

Las pupilas del hombre
fueron las ahijadas de la lluvia.
Las que vieron crecer el brote nuevo
entre altas humedades,
las que hallaron el goce
plácido, el goce puro de sólo estar oteando
cómo del bosque al río, por una red de lianas,
los dioses renovaban sueño con sueño el mundo,
y el vientre de la tierra
crecía en la estación hasta el milagro.

En los ojos del niño
se acumuló un invierno, el más pequeño,
el más profundo acaso,
porque los suaves pozos de su candor, llegaban
hasta la playa de otros mundos.

Así, llorar, era decir el ultramar del sueño,
tender un puente de agua sobre dos islas firmes,
amarrar a los hombres a su origen de niebla,
trazar la curva insólita de los advenimientos.

Este pequeño invierno todavía se asoma en los patriarcas.

Aún se conserva puro
como en la madrugada de la flor del camino.

Lo veis en los mercados
cuando un varón platica lentamente
y sale por su boca
la procesión de los antepasados que regresan
de la distante patria, a los oídos
del aire, del terrón, del heredero.

Winter of Man

At first, in the bitter ardors of the drouth,
the pupils of man
burned the images
inventing phantoms of ashes,
sterile gardens,
roses of lime,
garlands of fallen foliage.

The pupils of man
were godchildren of the rain.
They spied the growth of the new sprout
among high moistures,
they discovered placid
joy, the pure joy of simply observing
how from forest to river, along a net of vines,
the gods were renewing the world dream by dream,
and the earth's womb
increased in the season until the miracle.

In the child's eyes
a winter gathered—the smallest,
the deepest, perhaps,
because the soft wells of his candor reached
the shores of other worlds.

Thus, to cry was to say the realm of dream across the seas,
to stretch a bridge of water over two firm islands,
to fasten men to their origin of mist,
to trace the unusual curve of advents.

This small winter still appears in patriarchs.

It is still pure
as at the dawn of the flower in the path.

You see it in the marketplace
when a youth is speaking slowly
and there emerges from his mouth
the ancestral procession returning
from the distant homeland to the ears
of the wind, of the clod, of the new heir.

Pero no es fácil verlo. Es necesario
llorar, llorar desde la sangre misma
durante muchas lunas.

Lavar la vista en fuego,
en sal,
en aire,
hasta que el río del dolor nos muestra
su estremecido brazo.

But it isn't easily seen. It only comes by crying,
through crying from the blood itself
through many moons.

By washing sight in fire,
in salt,
in air
until the river of suffering shows us
its quivering arm.

Yo soy esta conciencia.

Esta manera simple de estar en la ventana
viendo llover.

Esta diaria agonía
de preguntar, y preguntarme el mundo,
la verdad,
el dominio invisible,
y anochecer sin nada entre las manos.

Yo soy esta conciencia, enarbolada
sobre el asta que el pez y la serpiente
y el lagarto y el pájaro y el mono
fueron labrando para mí.

Y adentro,
abajo,
en la caverna de los siglos,
toda la zoología me custodia los gestos.

Pero la zoología fue en el árbol,
y vivió de la luz de las naranjas
y el color de las hierbas.
Su sangre tiene sueño y clorofila.
Tiene cotiledones en el sexo,
yemas en el amor,
brotes menudos,
una sustancia de hoja bajo el cuerpo.

Mirad que el maíz vino de las aguas,
abuelas nuestras,
únicas paridoras del mundo,
y en su vaivén los siglos nos hallaron hundidos,
simplemente, esperando.

Del agua, por la roca, al primer musgo fino.
Del musgo, por el árbol, a la bestia desnuda.
De ella, por las torturas implacables del tiempo,
hasta el don de sabernos dioses desamparados,
lágrimas de los dioses,
invierno de los dioses
lloviendo nuestra lluvia de fatiga sin término.

I am this consciousness.

This simple way of being at the window
watching it rain.

This daily anguish
of asking, and being asked by the world,
about the truth,
the invisible authority,
and of seeing night come with nothing between my hands.

I am this consciousness, raised
from the mast that the fish and serpent
and lizard and bird and monkey
were fashioning for me.

And within,
below,
in the cavern of the centuries,
the whole zoological kingdom watches over my gestures.

But the zoological garden was in the tree,
and lived on the light of oranges
and the color of grasses.
Its blood was dream and chlorophil.
The embryo leaf was in the sex,
the yolk buds, in love,
tiny sprouts,
a leafy substance beneath the body.

Behold how the corn came from the waters,
our grandparents,
unique bearers of the world,
and how the centuries, hurrying by, found us submerged,
simply waiting.

From the water, through the rock, to the first delicate moss.
From the moss, through the tree, to the naked beast.
From it, through the implacable tortures of time,
to the gift of knowing ourselves to be helpless gods,
tears of the gods,
winter of the gods
raining our rain of endless fatigue.

De noche es el invierno como un dios desolado.
Miseria. Espacio enorme
cruzado por jaurías de viento, por bandadas
de miedos increíbles y opresiones oscuras.

Caen sobre el silencio
tambores pertinaces. La brujería cruza
sus maleficios, trenza sus palabras diabólicas,
amontona las nubes contra el insomnio,
enciende
las lámparas del trueno, fugaces y terribles.

Y entonces,
¡qué pequeños nosotros, desvalidos
bajo el sonoro palio de la tiniebla en brama!

El asombro camina descalzo por la alcoba.
Dice conjuros nimios,
impotentes conjuros,
exorcismos pequeños ante el pavor que cae quemando de la altura.

No hay amor.
No hay sollozo sino alarido puro,
del tamaño preciso de nuestra firme angustia.
No hay clemencia.
No hay trino.
No hay consuelo.
No hay mundo.

Sólo el puñal de un desamparo, hundido.

Winter is at night like a desolate god.
Misery. Enormous space
laced by hounds of the wind, by bands
of incredible fears and dark oppressions.

Upon the silence
fall persistent drums. Witchcraft stirs its mixture
of evil spells, twists together its diabolical words,
piles up the clouds against insomnia,
ignites
the terrible, streaking thunder lamps.

And then,
how small we are, how helpless
beneath the sonorous canopy of the embroiled darkness!

Amazement strolls barefoot through the bedroom
entoning trivial incantations,
impotent spells, small
exorcisms before the burning dread falling from the heights.

There is no love,
no sob, only a pure howl
the exact fit for our firm anguish.
There is no clemency,
no trill,
no consolation.
There is no world.

Only the dagger of helplessness, plunged deep.

Cante el varón su ascenso
desde el vientre infinito de las aguas.
Sus oceánicas células. Sus limos.
Sus iniciales lágrimas.

Cante el varón ahora
su arborescente lucha con la altura.

Su condición de pájaro
líquido y transparente.

Su sed del aire puro, que iba a llegar un día
a bendecir las branquias,
los pulmones,
la inspiración, la expiración del alma.

Cante todo el origen:
sus amnióticas fuentes congregadas
en donde nace el turbio río de los tiempos,
y el afán, el afán, la gran tortura
que lo alzó hasta el furor de las palabras,
lo hizo construir pirámides,
altas torres,
escalas,
maneras increíbles de endiosar su miseria,
de abrir puertas y cielos
y más cielos
y el oscuro recinto de la Nada.

Cante el amor, mitad de los caminos,
sitio exacto en que el viaje
abre su extraña flor,
copa perfecta
de la embriaguez perfecta,
cifra pura
de la exacta unidad y el doble impulso.

Cante la compañera de su sueño,
poco después nacida entre las páginas
de los mismos recuerdos:
la que brotó para las suavidades,
trajo perfume y sombra en los cabellos,
reposo y miel, asombro y esperanza.

50

Let man sing of his ascent
from the waters' infinite womb.
The oceanic cells. The slime.
The initial tears.

Let man now sing
of his arborous struggle with the heights.

His condition as a bird,
liquid and transparent.

His thirst for pure air, that one day was to arrive
to bless his branchia,
his lungs,
his breath, his expiring soul.

Let him sing of all origin:
its amniotic fountains pooled
where the turbid river of the ages is born,
and zeal, zeal, the great torture
that lifted it to the furor of words,
made it construct pyramids,
high towers,
ladders,
incredible ways to deify his misery,
to open doors and heavens
and more heavens
and the dark corner of Nothingness.

Let him sing of love, midpoint in the path,
precisely at the place where journey
opens its rare flower,
perfect cup
of complete euphoria,
pure cipher
of precise oneness and double impulse.

Let him sing of the companion of his dream,
born shortly thereafter between the pages
of the same memories:
the one that grew for softnesses,
endowed hair with perfume and shadow,
repose and honey, amazement and hope.

¿Quién eras tú, mujer, cuando las aguas
aprendían su don de transparencia?

¿Quién cuando el vendaval se sacudía
la espuma en el cenit de la tormenta?

¿Quién cuando Hunapúh
cortaba las mazorcas primigenias
y amasaba mi carne, en el reducto
de las más densas nieblas?

¿Quién cuando tuve voz para llamarte,
ojos para mirar cómo tu lámpara
iba a encender las lumbres de la tierra?

Cante el varón tu vientre
estremecido de generaciones,
árbol redondo de un millón de frutos,
puerto de nuevos vientres y varones.

Who were you, woman, when the waters
were learning their talent for transparency?

Who, when the windstorm was shaking off
the foam at the zenith of the storm?

Who, when Hunapúh
was cutting the primitive ears of corn
and kneading my flesh in the leftovers
of the densest clouds?

Who, when I received a voice to call you,
and eyes to see the manner of your lamp
igniting the luminaries of the earth?

Let man sing of your womb
aquiver from generations,
rotund tree of a million fruits,
harbor for new wombs and new men.

Toda la historia cabe en tus caderas,
mundo perfecto,
almendra de los sueños,
pluma multicolor de la alegría,
jade inocente,
suave espuma,
flor de acompañamiento,
huacal redondo,
jícara madura,
amanecida grácil de la estrella,
trozo de la esperanza,
promesa largamente silenciosa,
hierba del monte,
luz de las mazorcas.

Toda la historia cabe en tu regazo,
vientre fecundo,
mano acariciante,
tez de manzana-rosa,
cabello de obsidiana devanada
nixtamalero rútilo,
aroma vegetal,
sahumerio fino,
humus de los milagros,
renovación perenne de la raza.

Todo el amor te cabe en los oídos,
laberintos de asombro,
caracoles,
cuevas morenas,
musgos de deleite,
casas de la ilusión y del espasmo,
nidos de melodía,
barrancas del silencio despeñado,
tambores de avidez,
hondos estuches del susurro.

All history lies within your thighs,
a perfect world,
almond of dreams,
multi-hued plume of joy,
innocent jade,
delicate foam,
flower of companionship,
round huacal-vessel,
ripe jícara-cup,
slender dawn of the star,
parcel of hope,
promise longly hushed,
grass of the countryside,
corn tassels' light.

All history lies within your lap,
fecund womb,
hand for caress,
rose-apple complexion,
hair of swirled obsidian,
radiant nixtamalero for dough,
vegetal aroma,
fine aromatic incense,
humus of miracles,
perennial renewal of the race.

All love lies within your ears,
labyrinths of amazement,
shells of the sea,
dusky caverns,
mosses for delight,
homes of illusion and spasm,
nests for melody,
cliffs of the silence thrust down,
drums of eagerness,
deep recesses for whisper.

Todo el dolor te cabe en las pupilas,
piedra de los volcanes,
semillas de pacún,
granos de noche,
brillo de las albercas escondidas,
pozos de dulce pena,
congregación de lágrimas,
joyas vivas de luz,
espejos de la sombra,
carbones torturados,
brasa de la ternura sin orillas.

Toda la raza cabe en tu presencia,
cauce del tiempo,
río sin desmayo,
collar de muchas cuentas,
mazorca innumerable,
estero silencioso,
guardiana de los gestos,
patrona de rituales renovados,
custodia del futuro,
portera de las puertas de la tierra,
protectora morena,
madre de madres hasta el fin del mundo.

All suffering lies within your pupils,
flint of the volcanos,
seeds of the soapberry,
grains of night,
sparkle of hidden pools,
wells of sweet sorrow,
reservoir of tears,
vibrant jewels of light,
mirrors of the shadow,
tortured coals,
ember of unbounded tenderness.

All the race lies within your presence,
the channel for time,
river undaunted,
necklace of many beads,
numerous kernels of corn,
the silent marsh,
custodian of gestures,
pattern for rituals renewed,
guardian of the future,
gatekeeper of the earth's portals,
dark protectoress,
mother of mothers until the earth's end.

Invierno de la raza

El aire, un río largo que nace en la montaña
entre las rocas bravas,
como un cachorro de coyote, aúlla tristemente
y hace la noche densa
de miedos,
de rumores entrecortados,
taza de leches agrias,
panal lleno de avispas,
corazón sin sosiego.

Nosotros, en la noche,
heridos por la espada transparente del frío,
cubiertos por la sombra sagrada,
preparamos los últimos sacrificios del llanto.

Lejos. Todo está lejos. Terriblemente lejos.

El origen. La muerte. La realidad secreta de los dioses.

Los niños que se fueron
con el pecho rajado por la oración del pueblo,
en el humo, entre el humo, ya de humo,
copales
tiernos,
copales
inocentes, azulados,
con las manos alzadas
entre densos y amargos aromas de teocalli.

Las vírgenes donosas
cuyos sayales eran relámpagos de plumas
de papagayo,
cuyos güipiles eran también de aire y colores,
cuyas sonrisas eran, al final, tan dolientes.

Los guerreros cansados
bajo el granizo heroico de la muerte obsidiana,
los del paso vibrante,
la piel tensa,
los henchidos pulmones como teponahuastles,
los ojos en un fuego de volcanes fundidos.

Winter of the Race

The air, a lengthy river born in the mountain
between savage rock,
mournfully howls like the coyote cub
and charges the night dense
with fears
and faltering murmurs,
a cup of sour milk,
a honeycomb aswarm with wasps,
a disquieted heart.

We, in the night,
wounded by transparent swords of the cold,
shrouded in sacred shadow, prepare
the final sacrifice of waters of lament.

Distant. All so distant. Terribly distant.

Origin. Death. The secret verity of the gods.

Young boys who have gone,
breasts slashed by the prayer of the people,
in the smoke, within the smoke, already smoke,
tender
incense,
innocent copal,
bluish,
with hands uplifted,
amid heavy, acrid teocalli aromas.

Graceful virgins,
whose homespuns were lightning flashes of plumes
of parrot,
whose underskirts were güipiles of colors and air,
whose smiles were, finally, so sorrowful.

Wearied warriors,
under the heroic hail of obsidian death,
those with vibrant step,
taut skin,
lungs inflated like teponahuastles,
eyes with the fire of blazing volcanos.

Lejos. Todo está lejos. Terriblemente lejos.

El aire se ha llevado nuestro sosiego.
Ha sido cruel. No escucha nuestras viejas plegarias
ni se conmueve ante la danza
ni se detiene ante el conjuro.

Ahora
preparamos los últimos sacrificios del llanto.

¡Ah, poderosos guardianes de las puertas del agua!
¡Ved cómo están los estanques vacíos,
dormidas las acequias
por las cuatro esquinas del mundo,
secos los alimentos
y el sol, lagarto herido, yace sobre las piedras!
¡Abrid, pues, las compuertas!
¡Anegad esta sed, como una herida larga!
¡Verted la sangre fértil de los dioses
en el huacal tostado de la tierra!

Distant. All so distant. Terribly distant.

In its cruelty the air has carried away our calm.
It neither hears our ancient petitions
nor is moved by dance
nor is deterred by chant.

Now
we prepare the final sacrifice of waters of lament.

Oh powerful guardians of the flood gates!
See how empty are the pools!
How drowsy the streams
in the earth's four corners,
how withered the harvest,
and the sun, an injured lizard, lies upon the stones!

Throw open the gates!
Drench this thirst like a lingering wound!
Pour the fertile blood of the gods
into the scorched vessel of the earth's huacal!

Yo estuve aquí,
pinchándome con espinas de cardo,
hundiendo las agujas de maguey en la carne
sin alterar un músculo del rostro.

Me llené los cabellos
con el licor sagrado del más alto y tremendo sacrificio.

Dije las oraciones
aprendidas en cuevas de silencio.

Los Abuelos no oían.

Son viejos.

Son tan viejos
que el tiempo mismo no recuerda
si presenció su advenimiento, o ellos
vieron nacer al tiempo con ojos impasibles.

Continuó la sequía sobre los campos.
Vino
la sed, secando el verde lacerado del monte,
abriendo grietas con sus dedos rígidos
y levantando polvaredas contra el hambre del mundo.

Era que los Abuelos
nos decían con su voz más secreta:

"Fuisteis de lodo, y os faltó el impulso.
No alabasteis las manos que os dieron forma y sitio.

Fuisteis de la madera de los bosques,
de la resina del ocote fragante,
tuvisteis voz, y no loasteis
las manos que os tallaron.

Fuisteis, en la tercera creación de la vida,
hechos de la materia soñolienta
que duerme
entre las yemas rojas de las flores del pito,
y ni una sola voz
se alzó de vuestro sueño soterrado
para decir las manos que os trajeron al mundo.

I was here,
pricking myself with thorns of thistle,
plunging the cactus needles into my flesh
my face held immobile.

I soaked my hair
in sacred liquor of the most exalted, terrible sacrifice.

I said the prayers
learned in caverns of silence.

The Grandparents did not hear.

They are old.

They are so old
time itself does not remember
if it witnessed their coming, or if they
with their impassive eyes saw time being born.

Drought continued over the land.
Thirst came,
drying the blighted green of the countryside,
opening wide its cracks with rigid fingers,
raising duststorms against the hunger on earth.

For the Grandparents
told us with their voices of mystery:

"You were made of clay and you lacked impulse.
You praised not the hands that gave you form and place.

You were made of woods of the forest,
of resin of the fragrant ocote,
you were given voice and you did not laud
the hands that shaped you.

You, in the third creation of life,
were made of dream matter
that slumbers
amid crimson buds of the pito flower;
not a single voice
would rise from your secret dream
to say the hands that bore you into the world.

Hoy, hechos de maíz,
construidos en el horno trémulo de los dioses
con la más rica fécula,
hoy,
estatuas modeladas
con la sustancia pura de la vida,
hoy,
alimento entero,
también os olvidasteis del Abuelo y la Abuela.

Y no decís los días innumerables
que precedieron a los días.

Y no cantáis el calendario antiguo
que fue millones de años antes que las estrellas,
y miles de millones antes que la montaña,
y millón de millones conoció vuestra ausencia.

Tened, pues, el castigo.

Comed polvo. Llenaos los pulmones de polvo.
Que la boca renuente a la alabanza
se reseque de polvo".

Yo estuve aquí.
Quemando las resinas gratas a los Abuelos,
hablándoles con la voz humillada,
con los ojos heridos.
Pidiéndoles el más fértil regalo de las aguas.
Punzándome,
dolido alfiletero,
las carnes, ahora negras en licor de tortura.

Pasé el túnel del hambre, mascullando
oraciones
ensalmos,
toda la magia espléndida de los antepasados.

Y fue el horror:

¡Los Abuelos oyeron!

Today, made of corn,
taking form in the gods' tremulous oven,
with the richest starch,
today,
figures modeled
from the pure substance of life,
today,
a food replete,
you still forget the Grandmother and Grandfather.

You do not recount the innumerable days
that preceded the days.

You do not chant the ancient calendar
that was millions of years before the stars,
and thousands of millions before the mountain,
and a million millions knew of your absence.

Have, then, your punishment.

Swallow the dust. Fill your lungs with dust.
Let the tongue reluctant to praise
wither with dust."

I was here.
Burning resins pleasant to the Grandparents,
speaking to them with humbled voice,
with wounded eyes.
Seeking the most fertile gift of water.
Piercing myself,
suffering cushion
of flesh, now darkened by the liquor of torture.

I passed through the tunnel of hunger, muttering
prayers
psalms,
all the splendid magic of the ancestors.

And the horror was:

The Grandparents heard!

Bajando hacia el trasfondo de los sueños
yo te vi, sangre pura,
emerger de las grietas,
deslizarte por meandros subterráneos,
dibujar la serpiente,
el ala soñadora,
por los canales hondos de la raza.

Te vi surgir,
joya de los colores,
catarata de ardientes pitahayas,
para ir tallando el gesto decidido del hombre
y la tierna mirada que acompaña
su soledad madura.

Bajo los suelos blancos
que amasara la mano de los siglos
y el sol tostara en sus talleres de oro
—¡sangre de los valientes
sangre purificada de las vírgenes!—
te he visto fluir por rojos laberintos
y ascender,
lentamente,
de barro en barro,
de suspiro en lucha,
hasta los ojos ciegos de nuestros duros ídolos.

Si horadamos el mundo,
si buscamos la roca que yace ocultamente
bajo la roca,
y otra que está bajo esa roca,
si vamos desnudando toda la geología,
quitándole sus ásperos güipiles de basalto,
perforando volcanes
hasta donde palpitan los jades del comienzo,
hallaremos el río milenario,
el rubí de la fiebre
que da sustancia al hombre frente al aire.

Y allí también el mito.
Los dioses que existían antes que la palabra.
Los dioses que inventamos.
Los dioses que vendrán en los hombros del tiempo.

Traveling toward the underlining of dreams,
I saw you, pure blood,
emerge from the fissures,
glide through subterranean windings,
profiling the serpent
and the wing given to dreaming,
along the deep channels of the race.

I saw you surge forth,
jewel of the colors,
cataract of ardent pitahaya fruit,
carving out the determined grimace of man
and the tender glance that would accompany
his mature solitude.

Beside the whitened soils
kneaded by century's hand
scorched by the sun in its gold studios
—blood of the valiant,
purified blood of virgins!—
I have seen you flowing through red labyrinths
to ascend,
slowly,
from clay to clay,
from sigh to struggle,
up to the blind eyes of our hard idols.

If we burrow into the world,
if we search for the rock that lies in hiding
beneath the rock,
and another beneath that rock,
if we gradually denude all geology,
removing its coarse underskirts, güipiles of basalt,
drilling volcanos
down to the pulsing jades of the beginning,
we will find the millenial river,
the ruby of the fever
that affords man substance to face the air.

And there also the myth.
The gods that existed before the word.
The gods that we invented.
The gods that will come on the shoulders of time.

Allí el esbozo claro
de los pómulos,
el proyecto preciso del paso y la mirada,
la fuerza toda y su crueldad,
el llanto,
la fe como una espiga de maíz colorado,
¡todo lo que vivimos,
todo lo que nos forma sobre el llano del día,
todo lo que en el giro de los cielos, sangramos!

Un diluvio,
en los días que olvidaron los libros,
una lluvia incesante,
manchó de rojo vivo las escamas del viento,
repicó sobre el lomo de la tierra dormida
y empapó sus entrañas.
Se apozó en su silencio.

¡Ah, qué invierno de sangre,
lluvia de brasas líquidas!

Acaso fue la vena de los mitos
abierta en los teocallis invisibles del cielo.

Acaso un dios que amaba la futura presencia
del hombre,
dio su arteria
sacándose del pecho la rosa de la sangre.

Y ese invierno, hecho río, corre bajo las piedras.
Grita por la garganta seca de los volcanes.
Da razón a las milpas,
a la verde inocencia
del izote que eleva sus numerosas lámparas.
Ese invierno es la sangre del mundo,
de sus yerbas,
del insecto y el pájaro,
del pez,
de la leyenda.

There the clear outline
of the cheeks,
the precise plan for the step and the glance,
the tears of lament,
total strength and its cruelty,
faith like an ear of red corn,
all that we live
all that forms us upon the terrain of day,
all that in the turning of the heavens, we bleed!

A flood,
in days forgotten by the books,
an incessant rain,
stained vibrant red the scales of the wind,
stung the back of the sleeping earth,
and soaked its bowels.
It welled up in its silence.

Oh, what a winter of blood,
a rain of liquid embers!

Perhaps it was the vein of the myths
opened in the heavens' invisible teocallis.

Perhaps a god drawn to the future presence
of man
gave his artery
drawing from his chest the rose of the blood.

And that winter, become a river, runs beneath the stones.
It bellows through dry throats of volcanos.
It affirms the cornfields
and the green innocence
of the izote-yucca with its numerous lamps uplifted.
That winter is the blood of the world,
of its grasses,
of the insect and the bird,
of the fish,
of the legend.

Tenemos hoy todo el invierno a cuestas.
Todo el pasado, lleno de iniciales poderes,
jadeante,
irrepetible,
ferozmente presente
en los surcos que el llanto nos hizo en las mejillas.

Somos el mismo barro de ayer.
La misma máscara.
Pero ahora ya sabios de fatiga y silencio.

Nos talló el huracán.
Los dioses altos
nos dieron para el rostro su dolorido ejemplo.
La marca de su angustia señaló nuestro rictus.
Ya somos levadura para el pan de los muertos.

Porque todo el invierno
es esta joyería
que surge cuando alzamos la luz de los recuerdos.
Es el amor marchito.
Es el paso inseguro.
El lago de cansancio que en las pupilas queda
cuando ya los flechazos del verano
redujeron a sombras nuestros antiguos sueños.

Esto es: un lento viaje
por las ramas de sangre que en la raza se afincan.
Este venir de agobio por el ser de la historia
tocando una por una las vértebras del tiempo.

Fuimos niños ayer.
cuando empezaba
a germinar su chispa de cobalto
la luciérnaga errante.
Cuando el viento tenía
sin mancha alguna su sandalia virgen,
cuando todo el futuro,
como una fruta nueva,
esperaba los dientes golosos de la vida.

We bear today the whole of winter upon our backs.
All the past, filled with initial powers,
breathless,
unrepeatable,
fiercely present
in the furrows, waters of lament engraved into our cheeks.

We are the same clay of yesterday.
The same mask.
But now wise with fatigue and silence.

The hurricane shaped us.
The high gods
bestowed upon us their sorrowful example for a face.
The sign of their anguish marked our grimace.
We are now leaven for the bread of the dead.

Because all of winter
is this store of jewels
surging forth as we lift up memories' light.
It is the faded love,
the uncertain step,
the pool of weariness still in the pupils
when arrows of summer have finally
reduced to shadows our ancient dreams.

So it is this: a slow journey
along blood branches that settled in the race.
It is this exhaustion as history's very being
touches the vertebrae of time one by one.

We were children yesterday.
When the wandering firefly
began germinating
its spark of cobalt.
When the wind maintained
its virgin sandal without a stain,
when all the future,
like a new fruit,
awaited life's eager teeth.

Hoy, como las heroicas rocas de los comienzos,
tallados por el agua vertical de los siglos,
somos la imagen pétrea de la sabiduría,
la raza que desciende
al altar subterráneo de los humus vitales.

Y adentro,
en el regazo de la madre perfecta,
donde el maíz futuro prepara sus raíces,
donde el gusano borda sus túneles secretos,
nosotros,
con los dioses,
con la sabiduría,
con el logrado cúmulo de incontables inviernos,
alzaremos la raza nuevamente en el mundo,
su bandera,
su ímpetu,
su indefinible rostro de barro milenario.

Sabed, pues, la razón nunca antes dicha,
de este silencio nuestro.
Es el recogimiento de todas las palabras,
Es el recogimiento del puma para el salto
mortal,
vital,
que nos exige
la fiel perpetuidad de los inviernos.

Today, like the heroic rocks of the beginnings,
shaped by the vertical water of centuries,
we are the stone image of wisdom,
the race that descends
to the subterranean altar of vital humus.

And within,
nestling in the perfect mother,
where future corn prepares its roots,
where the worm embroiders its secret tunnels,
we—
with the gods,
with wisdom,
with the accomplishment of countless winters,
we will lift the race again in the world,
its banner,
its impetus,
its inscrutable face of millenial clay.

Discover, then, the reason never before given,
for this silence of ours.
It is the withdrawal of all words.
It is the withdrawal of the puma for the leap—
the fatal,
vital leap
that we are forced to fulfill
by the perennial faithfulness of the winters.

Invierno de la muerte

Hemos pasado ya por otras estaciones.

Por la estación de jade
en la que el coro de los días
era una guirnalda de yemas entreabiertas
y nosotros teníamos
el jugo fresco de los pinos.

Entonces, todo era un juego de palabras y sueños
que disparamos
hacia el futuro
y su sagrado rincón de profecía.

Después, la estación de oro
con su rueda de soles, su potencia de espigas promisorias,
su duro estío
tallado con el fuego de la luz más desnuda.

Por entonces,
el pulso fue certero, y el ojo
ganaba las batallas del distante horizonte,
y nuestra estampa era
como la de los príncipes sabios y valerosos.

Luego fue la estación de la cosecha:
el rico estuche del cacao,
el tabaco de la vena magnífica,
el humo como nido de congregados ritos y congojas,
como mar,
como nube de esperanzas distintas.

Por entonces
alzamos a la orilla del mundo
el templo,
el rancho oscuro, íntimo, donde el hijo
la mujer,
el comal,
la piedra silenciosa de moler, la fogata,
todo aprendió a vivir junto a nosotros.

Winter of Death

We have already passed through other seasons.

Through the season of jade
in which the chorus of days
was a garland of yolks partially opened
and we possessed
the fresh juice of the pines.

Then, everything was a game of words and dreams
that we sent shooting
toward the future
and its sacred corner of prophecy.

Then, the season of gold
with its wheel of suns, its potency of promising buds,
its harsh summer
shaped in the fire of naked light.

At that moment,
the pulse was certain, and the eye
was winning the battles of the distant horizon,
and our portrait was
like that of wise, worthy princes.

Then came the harvest season:
the rich pod of the cocoa,
the tobacco of superb vein,
the smoke like a nest of congregated rites and complaints,
like a sea,
like a cloud of different hopes.

At that moment,
we raised to the edge of the earth
the temple,
the dark, intimate hut where the son
the wife,
the comal,
silent grinding stone, the hearth fire,
all learned to live beside us.

Y hoy el invierno.
El día en que en los cielos
cierra Quetzalcoatl su pulsera de plumas.

El día en que los días
descienden al origen de la semilla intacta.

Somos nosotros, hoy, la misma lluvia.

Son las generaciones
que van cayendo, gota sobre gota,
sobre la tierra seca. Es el invierno
sin más agua que el agua de la sangre
despeñada por cauces de heroísmo
o alzada hasta los dioses en la entrega
ritual.

O sin más agua
que el llanto de las madres y los hijos
que nos vieron caer entre relámpagos
o a las serenas luces de la tarde.

And today, the winter.
The day in the heavens when
Quetzalcoatl closes his bracelet of feathers.

The day when the days
descend to the origin of the pristine seed.

We, today, are the same rain.

The generations
that gradually fall, drop upon drop,
over the dry land. Winter
without water other than the water of the blood
cast down through channels of heroism
or lifted to the gods in ritual
deliverance.

Or without other water
than the lament of the mothers and children
who saw us falling among lightning flashes
or in the serene lights of the afternoon.

Dormiremos aquí
donde la hormiga
acumula su sórdida riqueza.

Aquí,
donde el verano no se atreve
a hincar la azada
ni a plantar la flecha.

Aquí donde el festón de las raíces
se agazapa y enreda.

Dormiremos.

Donde el agua inefable del invierno
se filtra
leve, queda,
hasta mojar los párpados
y la sonrisa yerta.

Aquí,
taller sombrío en que se forjan
las cosechas.

Dormiremos aquí.

Cerrad la puerta.

We will sleep here
where the ant
accumulates its sordid riches.

Here,
where winter dares not
sink a hoe
nor plant an arrow.

Here where the festoon of roots
crouches down and twines around.

We will sleep.

Where the ineffable water of the winter
filters
lightly, quietly,
until it moistens the eyelids
and the frozen smile.

Here,
in the somber studio where harvests
are forged.

We will sleep here.

Close the door.

Sí: bajará la raza morena los peldaños
que de la luz conducen, por caminos de tiempo, al vientre de la mina.

Conocerá el silencio tenaz de los gusanos
y sabrá del oscuro poder que se concentra en las semillas.

Verá cómo los dioses, en ocultos palacios,
amasan los fermentos, las levaduras hondas que han de formar la vida.

Regresarán los huesos a su patria de altares subterráneos,
el corazón al pulso con que apenas palpitan las rocas primitivas.

Y desde allí, del fondo del sueño congregado,
en la comarca lenta de agazapados jugos, de nuevo concebido,
volverá a levantarse por escalas de asombro, hasta el nombre y amparo
de otro nahual más fuerte, más deslumbrante y sabio que el que fue su
padrino.

La raza irá por siglos sucumbiendo y alzándose.
Sucumbiendo y alzándose, crecerá por los siglos.
El quetzal ha de darle su libertad de selva, de arcoiris, de pájaro,
la serpiente emplumada, la virtud, el secreto que guardan sus anillos.

Yes: the dark-haired race will travel down the steps
that lead from light through time's paths to the mine's womb.

It will meet the tenacious silence of the worms
and will know of the dark power amassed in the seeds.

It will see the manner of the gods, how in hidden palaces,
they knead the ferments, the deep yeasts that will form life.

The bones will return to their country of subterranean altars,
the heart to the slight pulse of the primitive rocks.

And from there, from the backdrop of the dream that appeared
in the slow region of crouching juices, newly conceived,
it will rise up again on stairs of amazement, up to the name and
        guardianship
of another stronger, more dazzling, wiser nahual than its godfather.

For centuries the race will continually succumb and rise again.
Succumbing and rising, it will grow through the centuries.
The quetzal will give it his freedom of jungle, of rainbow, of bird,
the plumed serpent will give it virtue, the secret kept by his rings.

Invierno de los dioses

Gota a gota los astros
hacen caer sus fuegos amarillos.

Gota a gota los cielos
adornan de sortijas los dedos de la noche.

El surtidor que brota de las altas tinieblas,
gota a gota nos llena
de elemental asombro.

Es el invierno
de la luz.

La caída vertical de sus lámparas.
La siembra de luceros en el pecho del mundo.
La parábola roja.

El esplendor que intenta
repetir los caminos silenciosos del agua.

Mirad hacia la esquina más oculta del aire,
hacia la mancha negra
donde los dioses niños, acuclillados, ríen
y hacen rodar los globos de su alegría simple,
gota a gota
en el valle de la atmósfera inmensa.

Son ellos,
los pequeños, irresponsables dioses,
que juegan al invierno desparramando luces,
gozosos con el fuego redondo,
con la chispa,
con la mirada atónita de nosotros los hombres.

Arriba,
arrinconados dulcemente en la sombra,
¿qué palabras pronuncian,
qué mundos imaginan,
en qué misterios sueñan,
qué cosechas inventan con las semillas rubias?

Winter of the Gods

Drop by drop the stars
force their yellow fires to fall.

Drop by drop the heavens
adorn with ringlets the fingers of the night.

The fountain that sprinkles from the lofty darkness,
fills us drop by drop
with elemental amazement.

It is the winter
of the light.

The vertical waterfall of its lamps.
The sewing of star lights on the earth's breast.
The red parabola.

The splendor that seeks
to repeat the waters' silent paths.

Look toward the darkest corner of the air,
toward the black stain
where childgods, squatting on their heels, laugh
and make their simple joy balloons roll,
drop by drop
into the valley of the immense atmosphere.

They
are small, irresponsible gods,
that play at winter, scattering lights,
joyous with the rotund fire,
with the spark,
with the stunned glances of us, man.

Above,
huddled neatly in the shadow,
what words do they pronounce,
what worlds do they imagine,
what mysteries do they dream of,
what harvests do they invent with their blond seeds?

¡A llover,
a llover, luces pequeñas!

Para que el hombre gire como grano de asombro
en torno a innumerables universos,
gotas de luz
hechas del fuego de los juegos,
del entusiasmo de los dioses niños.

Y nosotros, abajo,
¿qué sacrificios puros tenemos,
qué oraciones,
qué manera de hablarles su lengua deleitosa,
para pedir que siempre,
gota a gota,
nos manden
su prodigioso invierno de estrellas disgregadas?

Rain,
rain, little lights!

So man may spin like a grain of amazement
around countless worlds,
drops of light
fashioned from the fire of games,
from the enthusiasm of childgods.

And we, below,
what pure sacrifices do we possess,
what prayers,
what ways to speak their delightful tongue,
for asking as always,
that they send us
drop by drop
their prodigious winter of exploded stars?

Luego vendrán por este mismo surco
los que tú y yo, mujer,
llamaremos a voces de rapto y agonía.

Llegarán a edificar nuevas ciudades,
a pulir otras rocas
y plantar otros árboles contra el muro del llanto.

Como un hilo de hormigas en el tiempo,
serán pacientes, duros,
y se hallarán ungidos
de nuestra milenaria fortaleza.

Sus manos alzarán de la tierra dormida
los dones del maíz
y el metal de las guerras necesarias.

Sus ojos
contra la imagen de la noche,
recogerán los gajos del renovado mito.
Y estarás otra vez entre mis sueños.
Cuerpo a cuerpo, luchando
la batalla perfecta de los hijos.
Beso a beso, mordiendo
la pulpa del amor, y delta a delta
—río doliente de la historia—
creando la sucesión de los afanes.

Para entonces
un siglo,
veinte siglos
y cien siglos de siglos,
tú y yo, la Raza, en repetida lluvia,
estaremos creciendo todavía.

Juntos, inevitablemente juntos,
subiremos por las gradas del templo
quemando pom,
pidiendo a los nahuales
por la brasa del chile,
por el incendio rubio de la chicha,
por el invierno pródigo y sus féculas,
por la sonrisa abierta de los campos
hecha mazorca entre las milpas fértiles.

Then along this very furrow will come
what you and I, woman,
will summon to us with voices of pleasure and agony.

Eventually they will build new cities,
polish other rocks
and plant other trees against the wall of lament.

Like a line of ants in time,
they will be patient and hard,
and they will be anointed
with our millenial strength.

Their hands will lift from the sleeping land
gifts of corn
and metal for the necessary wars.

Their eyes
to counter the image of the night,
will gather up the pieces of renewed myth.
And you will again be among my dreams.
Body to body, fighting
the perfect battle of the children.
Kiss to kiss, biting
the pulp of love, and delta to delta
—suffering river of history—
creating the succession of zeals.

So that later
in a century,
twenty centuries
a hundred centuries of centuries,
you and I, the Race, in repeated rain,
will still be growing.

Together, inevitably together,
we will ascend the steps of the temple
burning pom,
asking the nahuals
for the coal of the chili pepper,
for the blond fire of the fermented chicha,
for the prodigious winter and its starches,
for the open smile of the fields
become corn in the fertile milpas.

De tzolkín en tzolkín, de rueda en rueda,
de viento en viento cabalgante
sobre el redondo lomo de la nube,
de calendario en calendario,
viendo surgir montañas y apagarse mercados,
llegó siempre la lluvia
puntual, ansiosa, fértil
a coronar la cúspide solemne del teocalli.

Dialogó con los dioses.
Sobre el lejano cielo y el hombre dolorido.
Sobre las infinitas simientes que portaba
su mano de cristal, horrorosa y magnífica.

Acarició los rostros hieráticos
cuyas facciones eran la imagen fría del silencio.

Hizo rodar mil lágrimas por las máscaras quietas.
Cantó preces monótonas al pie de los altares.
Descendió por las gradas de la piedra antiquísima.
espejos de las plantas desnudas,
y pasó como líquida culebra, retorciéndose,
ensanchándose,
hundiéndose,
anillándose,
por los inacabables caminos de la historia.

From tzolkín to tzolkín, from wheel to wheel,
from wind to mounted wind
riding the rounded back of the cloud,
from calendar to calendar,
seeing mountains emerge and markets submerge,
punctual, anxious and fertile,
the rain always came
to crown the apex of the teocalli.

It conversed with the gods.
About the distant heaven and suffering man.
About the infinite seeds borne
by its magnificent, horrendous crystal hand.

It caressed the priestly faces
whose features were the cold image of silence.

It forced a thousand tears rolling down the quiet masks.
It sang monotonous praises at the foot of the altars.
It descended the steps of the ancient stone,
mirrors of the naked feet,
and it moved like a liquid serpent, writhing,
swelling,
submerging,
coiling,
along the endless pathways of history.

Translator's Note

The translation of *Maneras de llover* began with a few lines translated for the long critical introduction that precedes *Hugo Lindo: Sólo la voz/ Only the Voice*, Mundus Artium Press, 1984. In preparation for translating those forty-seven cantos I had read the total of Hugo Lindo's works: essay, prose fiction, and poetry. Correspondence with the author began in 1978 and continued until his death Sept. 9, 1985. Four years of research and refinement of translation versions toward recreating his poetic sensibility resulted in *Only the Voice*. The translation of *Maneras de llover* was guided principally by the understanding, gained in those years, of the aesthetic characteristics of Lindo's poetry and by conversation with the poet concerning the volume in my visit to El Salvador for the *homenaje* to the poet, November 18, 1984.

A thorough comprehension of an author's vocabulary, style, and manner of the text's dominant qualities, and of the technical devices employed in the text's structure must guide its translation. The multiple linguistic, aesthetic and cultural aspects involved in translating a book of poetry are voluminous. Hugo Lindo's poetry requires the translator's close attention to the lyrical, rhythmic qualities of the verse while preserving the metaphorical reference, content, structure and in many cases an almost Psalm-like tone.

In *Maneras de llover* the cultural context places special demands on the translator not only to understand it but also to carry over to the English speaker the meaning of native words without using distracting footnotes or destroying the tone and mood. I retained some native words to give an exotic flavor to the English text, a flavor which definitely exists for the reader of the Spanish. Some terms are not Castilian; a *güipil* is only worn in Central America and Yucatan. In this translation, the meaning is suggested through the addition of "skirts" or "underskirts," more appropriate than "dress" or "slip" as it is less likely to have urban resonance. *Teocalli* is not translated into "temple" because it appears in the English dictionary; also, the prefix "teo" is close to "deo," for god, and "temple" may not call up the Indian image in English; in the particular stanza of its initial use the meaning of *teocalli* may be indicated by its contextual nearness to "incense." As with the word *jícara*, a gourd or clay cup for chocolate, context must clarify the meaning since that meaning is of particular importance; in the translation the word "cup" was added. The "mocking song" of the *cenzontle* identified for the reader the mockingbird later mentioned only as a *cenzontle*.

The title, "The Ways of Rain," was chosen to conserve the serious tone, to carry the semantic level and also to allow the words to flow on the tongue. Of other possibilities, "Ways to Rain" is flat; "Ways of Raining" is more active, possibly more accurate, less elegant; "Manners of Raining" was Hugo Lindo's choice and is more pleasant in sound but less understandable than the title in Spanish: the first meaning of "manners" in English is different from that of *maneras*. "The Ways of Rain" seemed more fitting semantically within the context of the entire volume in which Rain and Winter are synonymous: in the seven winters Rain acts in various ways during the creation-life-death cycle; therefore, "The Ways of Rain," for me a soothing, gentle phrase, a compromise, for there is no equivalent.

Part of the problem of equivalency is due to resonance that is desired or not desired, as for example the word "temple," a perfectly good word except it does not produce the image of a *teocalli*. Perhaps this double problem of desired vs. undesired resonance is treated best in the first two poems in Lindo's *Fácil palabra*. -1- "Easy would the word be/ if it did not sprout leaves./ Easy like an empty space./ Like a shadow./ But the opposite occurs: you approach silence/ and it attacks you/ filled with ideas, with memories,/ always handling something./ and you simply do not attain it/ naked,/ alone." -2- "A word you pursue/ and it is not the word./ If you do find one, you find/ only a shell." In the case of the word *llanto* the problems of resonance are acute; *"llanto"* means copious "grieving," "weeping," "crying": "a flood of tears." Furthermore, the sonorous effect of *llanto* is not available in English: -ing words are not easily appropriated for pleasant sound; "flood of tears" might be considered florid or clichéd. *Llanto* has a relationship in Spanish with *lluvia* and *llover*, noun and verb for rain and used interchangeably by Lindo for crying, "we are raining our rain of fatigue" (canto two of "Winter of Man"). *Llanto* is used in various situations so that the mental, emotional connections will be destroyed in the translation unless some relationship is established between the words chosen. In my translation "waters of lament" introduces the metaphor in the first introductory canto. It is repeated in "in the furrows waters of lament engraved into our cheeks," *"en los surcos que el llanto nos hizo en las mejillas"* ("Winter of the Race") and "without other water/ than the lament of the mothers and children," *"sin más agua que el llanto"* (canto one "Winter of Death"). Waters of lament also establishes a relationship with "Of water," *"De agua,"* the refrain in the third canto of "Winter of the Rock," and with the rain and waters that pervade the poem. The fluid sound of the word "water" reinforces its image. In translating, the translator tries to substitute some positives for the unavoidable sacrifices.

Outstanding aspects of the volume *Maneras de llover* are vivid imagery and modulating movement coupled with appropriate linguistic sounds to provide the often rapidly changing mood of the poem. In concentrating on one of these facets of the text it would be easy for the translator to ignore other aspects. The translation must also be guided by the poet's aesthetic philosophy and structural methods or processes he uses to carry out his aesthetic intent. How these multiple linguistic and philosophic concerns are joined in the text can be illustrated by consideration of the translation of juxtaposed, opposing images in these lines: "I speak of the relentless winter,/ the savage, multiple fury/ in whose strokes is softened/ the air's transparent face." (Canto 2). It is important for the translator to know of the poet's strong focus on the dualistic aspects of life and to recognize the linguistic, poetic devices he uses to bring attention to that focus. As in the original text, the oppositions in this passage require vocabulary for the first two lines to be chosen for harshness which will counter the softness of the last two. In the translation the three hard beats "speak, relentless, winter," balance with "savage, multiple, fury"; these counter the balanced, gentle rhythm and sibilant sounds of the last two lines: "in whose strokes is softened/ the air's transparent face." In general, in the translation of this poem the rhythmic movement of the original text is preserved in part by retention of the quality of the verb, taking care not to substitute adjectives or passive verbs for active verbs.

The intent of this translator was to provide the English reader with an experience as similar to that of a reader of the original text as is possible. As has just been discussed, in order to accomplish this, the metaphorical and structural methods used by the poet were emulated in the English translation to try to recreate the style. The beauty of Hugo Lindo's poetry is a challenge of considerable proportions, but the act of translating became a joy (the joy expressed in the last lines of *"Entre palabras"* ("Between Words"): "replete wholeness that is near to pain" as the translator savored every word, sound and rhythm in the effort to recreate the mystery and magic of Hugo Lindo's *Maneras de llover*.[1]

[1]A full discussion of the translation of Hugo Lindo's *Sólo la voz* is in my essay "Retracing the Translation Process: Hugo Lindo's *Only the Voice*," in *Translation Review* 7 (1981): 32-40.

The Poetry of Hugo Lindo

The philosophical base and the essential stylistic character of Lindo's poetry do not vary from *Poema eucarístico y otros* in 1943 to his latest published work, *Fácil palabra* (Easy Word), 1985. However, each of the volumes is very different in content and thematic treatment, and his later volumes show a refinement of his artistic skills. In his poetry Hugo Lindo expresses an attitude of perplexity in facing the solitude and the grief in the world around him, along with a paradoxical affirmation of hope despite the negative aspects of the world about him. Although intensely personal, the mode is not confessional and Lindo's personal experience is always joined to the individual and collective human experience of others, often through the editorial "we" as in "The Memory of Spring": "I speak today about the rose/ because it is not expendable, because we must affirm it/ and affirm ourselves/ in its slender line." As seen in that example his style is straightforward and vigorous but not conversational, and his vocabulary is simple and crisp, with few flourishes. The tone of a poem will vary, often within a single stanza, from nostalgic, confident, pontifical, laudatory, psalmodic, to anxious, pleading, demanding or ironic. His metaphorical references range from those inspired by his particular cultural heritage in El Salvador to classical allusions and universal symbols; he frequently mixes their use. His images are concrete, but with figurative resonance, as in the "rose" just cited.

An example of many of these characteristics is found in these lines, written in his youth, from "The Dimension of Hope," 1943. The poet prays to the earth mother to "extinguish the scream/ of the mutilated man...": "Earth, withered and pompous mother,/ conquering and conquered mother, lap for the hyena and the butterfly,/ ...extinguish the scream." Then, the poet calls on "Our Father who art on earth" (not in Heaven) and states prophetically: "God will be with us down here./ And, placed on the other side of war,/ then we will pray, ... a prayer at the level of life:/ 'Our Father who art on earth...!' In these lines the poet's perplexity and affirmation are vividly expressed in symbolic concrete images using simple vocabulary. The Catholic and Indian heritage are juxtaposed. In such a juxtaposition Hugo Lindo expresses his sense of the unity of life: his poetry focuses on the individuality yet sameness of human experience, and it is conceived within an Oriental or Indian cyclical time frame rather than a historically chronological Western one. In like manner, the very nature of being is without regard to time and place, and, in his pantheistic view, is equally applicable to rock, tree, animal, and man: all share the contradictory experience of the pain and joy of existence. Therefore, aspects of nature, the light of day and the dark of night are used metaphorically for the exhilaration and despair felt by the human being.

Maneras de llover, first published in Spain in 1969, is written using the same techniques as Hugo Lindo's other books of poetry. However, the nature of the volume is very different, even from that of his other long poems. Hugo Lindo's other highly structured long poems are *Libro de horas* (Book of Hours), 1948, *Navegante río* (Sailing River), 1963, and *Resonancia de Vivaldi* (Resonance of Vivaldi), 1976. In these long poems the individual cantos are worthy poems in their own right although each is enhanced by its placement within the volume. *Resonancia de Vivaldi* was published in a deluxe, numbered edition with paintings by the Salvadoran Carlos Cañas. The cantos of this volume chant the four seasons.[1] *Sólo la voz* (*Only the Voice*), 1968, is a long, lyric poem but its structure is looser; its themes intertwine and individual cantos recall each other; through these devices the poem is unified and builds to a final climax. Each of the books mentioned follows the life cycle in a different way. *Poema eucarístico y otros* (Eucharist Poem and Others), 1943, is a book of several poems that also follow a definite patterned development.

Trece instantes (Thirteen Moments), 1959, *Sinfonía del límite* (Symphony of Limits), 1953, and *Sangre de Hispania fecunda* (Blood of Fecund Spain), 1972 are collections of individual poems, some of which are sonnets. Many of Hugo Lindo's sonnets have appeared in newspapers and journals and are not available in book form.

Este pequeño siempre (This Little Bit of Always), 1971, is a socially oriented volume. Each poem is dedicated to an individual friend or friends; some are poets and authors in different nations; all are facing the essential problems of the human condition: being individuals who love peace but also belong to the human community with its injustices and political extremes. The first poem in the book is dedicated to Hugo Lindo's poet son whom he addresses as "My son, my brother" (A Ricardo Lindo, hijo mío, hermano mío). In the poem they seek together their individual and collective identities against the background of "Planes dirtying the birds' air" and surrounded by confusion such that "I don't find my face at times in the face of my exploited brother, or see my hand in the hand that is strangling him." (No hallo mi rostro a veces en el rostro del hermano estrujado,/ ni veo a veces mi mano en la mano que lo estrangula.) Poems dedicated to Venezuelan poets and to Guatemalan poets are included in the present text among the selections from Hugo Lindo's other volumes of poetry.

Of the poems of *Fácil palabra* some were written in Madrid between the years of 1970 and 1972 when Hugo Lindo was ambassador to Spain, and many appeared in journals there. The rest were written in 1981 and 1982 at his home in San Salvador. Omission of a few poems from the original manuscript leaves the published collection with one hundred ninety-five brief poems thematically oriented toward the complexities of life and the difficulties of expressing the vital experience. Two poems from this volume quoted in the "Translator's Note" appear with others in "Selections from the Poetry of Hugo Lindo."

The poetry in manuscript, written in 1981 and 1982, "Prólogo a la noche" consisting of 30 poems and "Casi en la luz" of 32 poems, has been scheduled for publication in the *Colección Hugo Lindo Poesía*. The themes in "Prólogo a la noche" (Prologue to Night) are oriented toward impending death and insistence on a positive attitude, not in a Pollyanna sense nor with a didactic tone, but expressed in a frank, open manner. Though the tone may vary, the poems share the theme of the poem, "Six Lines," that concludes the collection: "Why when there is so much bitterness/ do you speak of the flower and the kiss/ harmony and bliss?/ Why when there is so much bitterness/ do you in your madness persist?/ —Precisely, because of this." The poems of "Casi en la luz" (Almost in the Light) seem more thoughtful and still more affirmative in philosophic stance. The poet views the wholeness of life experience and sees no boundary between life and death, as in "Nada" (Nothing) "the door was the same/ open or closed:/ a simple illusion." From "Casi en la luz" the poem dedicated to the translator, "Entre palabras," is included in "Selections...."

The poetry Hugo Lindo was writing at his death, entitled "Desmesura" (Unrestrained), covers the years from 1983 to September 1985. Nine thousand seven hundred thirty-three lines, some two hundred pages of manuscript, this long poem covers the range of life experiences important to the poet: his beliefs, his family, music through the ages, and certain authors and places, such as the poem to Granada; it is his ultimate effort to say all those things he felt he was pressured for time to say before his impending death. He began recording the poem but was unable to finish.

Characteristic of the aesthetic expression of all eleven volumes of Lindo's published poetry are clear, sometimes startling images, deceptive simplicity, and paradoxical questioning. As in *The Ways of Rain* the poet displays a mastery of suggestive imagery and contradictory metaphors, "lightning flashes of feathers of parrot,"and of juxtaposition of opposing images or situations, for example, "Origin. Death"; these techniques often provide an unsettling, shifting foundation for the reader. Rather than naming colors the poet may suggest them, as in "blazing volcanos," in which the vocabulary chosen conjures up the colorful image. The poem "De la poesía" ("On poetry") [in the "Selections from the Poetry of Hugo Lindo"] reveals this aesthetic goal of the poet: to suggest rather than to name. In this poem the intangible nature of poetry is dramatized by the juxtaposition of seemingly unrelated images. The poet's techniques force the reader's participation to attain a meaning that is not afforded through definition but through "hieroglyphics" that require imagination and intuition for interpretation. Although his long lyric poems are developed within an intellectual framework, the dramatic, visual and musical qualities remain dominant characteristics. For this reason his concepts surface without strain and because his poetic techniques, such as dynamic metaphors (example: "...suckled at abrasive nipples/ of the [volcano] Momotombo...") are consistent with his paradoxical vision.

The music of Lindo's poetry is best appreciated in oral reading. Lyricism is produced through strong interior rhythmic phrasing, sonorous vocabulary, repetitions and refrains that evoke shifting moods and modulating tones. These shifts are often unexpected and therefore may occasion surprise. The music is of such vigor that the reader may be carried by its sheer force. The cantos of *Sólo la voz* have been turned into music for acapella choir by the Salvadoran composer, Germán Cáceres, a former Guggenheim fellow. The music was performed in San Salvador in November of 1984 during an *homenaje* to the poet.

Perhaps the most essential characteristic of the poetry of Hugo Lindo is its consistency in spirit. The heart and soul of the poet are etched into every line of his poetry. That may be the reason Lindo's poetry rarely strikes an off note or seems contrived. The poems of Hugo Lindo evoke the world of Hugo Lindo with nostalgia and love and joy and suffering and a determined paradoxical affirmation. The poet may have best expressed the sacrificial nature of the love which sustained that affirmation in lines from his last poem, where the sea is used as an analogy from which a lesson can be drawn: The great book was the sea that was incessantly eliminating itself passing through the folds of the foam all feeling, the full scripture of love as the only reason in life. (Era el mar el gran libro que a sí mismo incesante suicidíase pasando por los folios de la espuma todo el sentir, la plena escritura del amor como la sola razón de vida.) "Desmesura," 1985.

[1] On June 18, 1983, Vivaldi's "Four Seasons," performed by the Ensemble of San Salvador directed by Germán Cáceres, was presented along with the reading of the poem by Isabel Dada.

Selections from the Poetry of Hugo Lindo

Selecciones de la poesía de Hugo Lindo

(1943-1985)

Selecciones de *Sinfonía del límite*

De la poesía

Bien: es lo que decíamos ahora.
Encenderse de lámparas sin motivo aparente.
Alzar copas maduras
y beber los colores de la nieve
como quien bebe alas de paloma
o brinda con angélicas especies.

Claro: lo que decíamos ahora,
¿Para qué detener en las palabras
lo que se va por ellas, y revierte
en el propio minuto del encanto
a su silencio tenue?
¿Para qué definir lo que pudiera
relatarse jeroglíficamente?

Exactamente: de eso hablábamos.
De no decir el nombre de las cosas
ni aquella calidad que las aprieta,
sino sólo su sombra,
mejor dicho, el milagro
sonoro de su aroma.
Dejar que las palabras
por sí solas
tomen hacia el prodigio
la ruta aérea de las hojas.

Selections from *Sinfonía del límite*

On Poetry

So: it is as we were saying.
A lighting of lamps without apparent reason.
Raising glasses of mellowed wine,
and drinking the colors of snow
as one who sips wings of the dove
or offers a toast with angels.

Certainly: as we were saying.
Why detain within words
what will slip through them and
at the very moment of the spell
revert into its tenuous silence?
Why define what may be
conveyed in hieroglyphics?

Precisely: we were just saying so.
Not to name the things or
any quality that constricts them
but rather their shadow,
the miraculous
resonance of their aromas.
So the words themselves
will travel toward the miracle
alone,
along the airways of the leaves.

Presencia del hoy

Hoy
soy.

Mi cifra secreta
se afirma en la grieta
presente
y potente
del hoy.

El poeta
se palpa y se siente
y se dice: soy.

Si he sido
o no he sido
ya está en el olvido;
si marcho, no sé.

Que todo el futuro
se halla en el más puro
lejano y oscuro
reducto de fe.

Hoy
soy.

Y me alzo en el día,
bandera
de fiebre y poesía.

Y en la noche grito
mi voz de quimera,
mi sed de infinito.

La garganta
canta,
la emoción acecha,
y el tiempo su flecha
detiene,
su aliento
contiene,
sus pulsos aquieta.

Presence of the Today

I say
I am, today

My secret cipher
affirms itself
in its present
potent crevice
of the today.

As the poet
gropes to feel his way,
to himself he can say, I am today.

If I've been
or haven't been
is now forgotten;
if I proceed, I can't say.

For all the future
lies within a distant, obscure,
and most pure
redoubt of faith.

I say
I am, today.

Daily I fly
a flag
of fever and poetry.

Nightly I scream
my voice of dream,
my thirst for infinity.

My throat
sings,
emotion lies in wait,
as time reins in
its dart,
restrains
its breath,
and calms its heart.

Hoy
soy.

El poeta
se afirma en la grieta
presente
y potente
del hoy.

Cabelleras de humo

Cabelleras de humo
en la danza redondo, los mundos.

Espirales de llama
en la danza redonda, las almas.

Ahora gira en el viento violento
sus aspas el Verbo.

Y se entrega la carne del Caos
al estupro vital del Milagro.

I say
I am, today.

For the poet
affirms himself
in the present
potent crevice
of the today.

Comets of Smoke

Comets of smoke
in a spherical dance, worlds.

Spirals of flame
in a spherical dance, souls.

Now whirling its arms in the violent wind,
is the Word.

And Chaos surrenders her flesh
to the vital rape of Miracle.

Conjugación del verbo ser

Yo soy, tú eres, él es...
En el aire se deshacen
los pronombres y los verbos
por la herida de la tarde.

Yo, tú, él, nosotros, todos
encadenados de márgenes:
cada uno es cada uno,
nadie es el otro ni nadie:
yo no soy tú, ni él es yo,
ni hay un corazón tan grande
que empuje por nuestras venas
la caridad de otras sangres...

Yo, tú, él...y nuestras casas
firmes de lodos y mármoles,
con puertas y con paredes,
ventanas y barandales...

Yo soy, tú eres, él es...
¡Que el verbo ser nos ampare
ahora que conjugamos verbos más puros y grandes!

Porque yo guardo memoria
de un tiempo de eternidades,
en donde todo era yo,
todo eras tú, y él, y nadie:
que las divididas casas
no tenían sus señales,
ni los arroyos corrían,
ni se encrespaban los mares,
ni las sombras de los cielos
inundaban las ciudades:
de un tiempo que no era tiempo,
de un todo que no era partes,
de un magnífico pronombre
sin cercos, muros ni alambres...

Conjugation of the Verb, to Be

I am, you are, he is...
The pronouns and the verbs
shatter in the air
wounded by the afternoon.

I, you, he, we, everyone
chained to limits:
each one is each one,
no one is another, nor anyone:
I am not you, nor is he, I,
nor is there a heart large enough
to drive through our veins
the benevolence of other bloods...

I, you, he... and our houses
firm in their mud and marble,
their doors and walls,
windows and railings...

I am, you are, he is...
May the verb, to be, assist us
now as we conjugate purer, greater verbs!

Because I retain a memory
of a time of eternities,
in a place where all was I,
all was you, and he and no one:
for the separate houses
had no addresses,
nor were the streams running,
nor were the seas cresting,
nor were the shadows of the heavens
flooding the cities:
of a time that was not time,
of a whole that was not parts,
of a wonderful pronoun
without enclosures, wires, or walls...

Yo soy, tú eres, él es...
Más allá de ti no hay nadie:
¿Quién te demuestra mi esencia?
¿Cómo tu pena me llague?
¿Por qué ruta su alegría
ha de llegar a tus valles?

La noche que se avecina
con sus amarillos cálices,
no aprendió las incompletas
verdades gramaticales:
ella es noche, porque no es:
porque la luz no la invade,
porque su callada pulpa
no es rota por los alfanjes,
porque no tiene riberas,
contornos, perfiles, madres:
porque discurre en sí misma
y en sí se completa y vale:
porque no es un yo ni un tú,
porque no es un él ni un nadie,
porque resume en sus ámbitos
el Todo inmenso, sin partes:
porque su aroma de estrellas
en los jardines del aire
no tiene nombres pequeños
en los pliegues de sus cálices.

Yo soy, tú eres, él es...
Nosotros NO SOMOS...
        ¡Abre
Adán, tu conciencia sorda!
¡Rompe el muro de tus carnes!
¡Sé tú, sé yo, y él, y todos,
de modo que nos ampare
una sola realidad
y un solo fuego nos marque!

I am, you are, he is...
Beyond you there is no one:
How is your sorrow to hurt me?
Who will teach you my essence?
Along what path must its joy
reach your valleys?

Night that draws close
with its yellow chalices,
did not learn the incomplete
grammatical truths:
she is night because she is not:
because light does not penetrate her,
because her silenced flesh
is not broken by the cutlass,
because she has no shorelines,
shapes, profiles, riverbed:
because she discusses with herself
and is complemented by herself and is worthy in herself:
because she is not an I nor a you,
because she is not a he nor an anyone,
because she encompasses in her expanse
the immense ALL, without parts:
because her aroma of stars
in the gardens of air
has no small names
in the flutes of her chalices.

I am, you are, he is...
We, WE ARE NOT...
Adam, open up
your dulled consciousness!
Break open the wall of your flesh!
Be yourself, be me, and him, and everyone,
so a single reality
will protect us
and a single fire will mark us!

Selecciones de *Trece instantes*

Amanecer

Está la gota de rocío
soñando tan sin motivo.

¡Ojo-luz de la mañana,
ojo del aire, ojo vivo!
Un aluvión de colores
se ha despeñado en su recinto,
y eso lo saben las abejas
y lo comprenden bien los niños.

Un ángel de terciopelo
duerme en el pétalo clarísimo
y los mil duendes de la infancia
doran la cumbre de un pistilo.
¡Ah, magia blanca y olvidada
en dulces tiempos fugitivos!

El ojo-luz ve mariposas
también de luz, y ve el camino,
y ve los árboles que empiezan
a bostezar, y el casarío
que despereza, soñoliento,
puertas, carretas, gallos, linos...

Selections from *Trece instantes*

Daybreak

The dewdrop is
dreaming, with so little reason.

Eye-light of the morning,
of the breeze, vital eye!
Torrents of colors
have plunged into your circle;
the bees are aware of this
and children know it well.

Upon the glistening petal
a velvet angel sleeps
and childhood's wondrous elves
brighten a pistil's peak.
A white magic now abandoned
in endearing, elusive times!

The eye-light sees butterflies,
fashioned of light, also,
and it sees the path, and the trees
as they begin to yawn,
the village stretching drowsily,
doorways, pushcarts, roosters, linens...

Un dios desnudo

Yo quiero crear un mundo
que tenga menos gravedad
y un alto acopio de alegría.

Aprender a mirar
el juego de las cosas
que hacen ronda en la luz
y oír el coro
de los árboles viejos en el campo,
de los amaneceres pueblerinos,
de las luchas del hombre.

Adivinad los ángeles que bailan
en un pecho de niña,
y el hilo del olvido que te teje
en el largo bostezo del poblado.

Venid conmigo a la región del sueño,
ebria de sinrazones,
y embriagáos también con las palabras
que el aire lleva en sus doradas cintas.

Ved, por ejemplo, un vidrio de colores,
perfectamente mágico.

La fila militar del hormiguero
como un trozo de historia.

El ojo de la alberca
azulmente asombrado.

Repetid con mi acento:
un dios desnudo
camina levemente por las cosas
y deja su alegría,
estela de fragancia, en el camino.

A Naked God

I want to create a world
that has less gravity
and more abounding joy.

To learn to watch
the things at play
as they circle in the light
and to hear the country choir
of aged trees,
dawning villages,
struggling men.

Guess what angels dance
within a child's breast,
what thread of forgetfulness is spun for you
in the open yawn.

Join me in the region of dream,
that is tipsy with nonsense,
and feel the intoxication of the words
breezes carry on their gold ribbons.

Observe, for example, a glass of colors,
perfectly magical.

The anthills' soldierly lines
like a piece of history.

The reservoir spring,
wondrous in its blue.

Entone with me:
a naked god
strolls amid the things
and leaves his joy behind,
a trail of fragrance, along the path.

La voz

Ser la ilusión precisa, descarnada,
la luz desnuda y el silencio puro.
Enarbolar secreto y fin maduro
en un fleco de niebla, en una espada.

Cantar la voz, la sola voz, y nada
más que la voz. Acaso el verbo duro.
Y ha de durar, en el aliento oscuro,
la voz sin adjetivo disfrazada.

Levantar la basílica del fuego
sobre mutable corazón de arena,
quemar en ella la ansiedad, y luego

sin más concepto que la propia llama,
encontrar que era dulce y era buena
la voz que íntimamente nos reclama.

The Voice

To become a true illusion, a bared,
naked light, to become a silence pure,
unfurling mystery and matured
concerns from tufts of cloud, on a rapier.

To entone the voice and thus to declare,
with the harsh verb, the voice to endure,
disguised by no adjective, the obscure
breath to carry the voice on waves of air.

To raise the basilica of scourging fire
upon an ever inconstant heart of sand,
to burn anxiety upon her pyre

then having no thought beyond the flame,
to find that what effected our reclaim
was the good, gentle voice dwelling within.

Selecciones de *Navegante río*

Sangre adentro

Como se entra en calor
yo voy entrando en sangre.

Primero por el peso de los párpados
y el ardor de los ojos.
Después, por el pequeño golpeteo a sordina
que hiere el yunque de las sienes.
Luego, por el reloj de las arterias
que va marcando el pulso de la vida,
y un fuego de rubor que sube al rostro
por la escalera dura de la fiebre.

Yo voy entrando en sangre.

Dejadla fluir
y que la boca de la herida cante.

Dirá pausadamente a los comienzos
lo que después ha de gritar a borbotones.

Empezará a correr como un hilillo
casi inocente
para inundar la historia
con su líquida lámpara y su esfuerzo.

Porque los dioses, los altivos dioses,
no tienen sangre.

Sólo nosotros, dioses disminuidos
o gusanos alzados.

Sólo nosotros, digo, con la marca y marea
de su flujo,
desde que era doncella nuestra madre,
desde que su amapola de ternura
se rasgó para darnos cal y canto,
desde que en el pulmón del primer aire
nuestro grito inicial abrió las puertas.

Selections from *Navegante río*

Inside Blood

As one coming into heat
I am coming into blood.

First through the eyelids' weight
and the eyes' warmth.
Then, through the muted tapping
that wounds the temples' forge.
Later, through the arteries' clock,
marking life's pulse,
and the fire of a blush that climbs to the face
up fever's hard ladder.

I am coming into blood.

Let it flow
and let the mouth of the wound sing.

At first, it will leisurely say
what will later gush out in a scream.

It will begin like an almost innocent
trickle
to flood history
with its liquid lamp and its strength.

Because the gods, the haughty gods,
have no blood.

Only we, diminished gods
or uplifted worms.

Only we, I say, with the mark and tide
of its flow,
since our mother's maidenhood
since her poppy of tenderness
was pricked to give us brick and mortar,
since our initial scream opened
the door to the lung of the first air.

¿O estaba nuestra sangre en otra sangre,
y desde ayer venía persiguiéndonos?
(De un color en el mar—sangre del mundo—,
de otro color entre las venas de los bosques).

¡Oh, sí! Yo soy mi sangre. Y ella empina
la sustancia del canto.

Vedla bajar por aluvión de siglos
hasta lengua y garganta,
a veces como amor, como tornado,
como pecho rajado por la guerra,
como víscera rota.

Vedla venir de los varones
y de las hembras del pasado,
en el torrente de una magia
creadora, inevitable.

¡Cuánta memoria de sonrisa y llanto!
¡Qué aglomerados miedos en su nombre!

Y el jardín de la muerte con sus flores
a medio abrir, abriéndose, ya abiertas,
para que el semen de los cementerios
edifique la sangre de los hijos.

Si el hombre navegara sangre adentro
y supiera el rumor de su congoja,
el gorgoteo de su instinto
y la burbuja de su pensamiento;
si el hombre, como un ojo sangre adentro,
viera su eternidad y su minuto
y la arista cabal de su destino,
sabría ya que hay una sola sangre,
la de los muertos y la nuestra, ardiendo.

Or was our blood in another blood,
pursuing us since yesterday?
Of one color in the sea —blood of the world—
of another color within the forests' veins.

Oh, yes! I am my blood. And it sips
the substance of song.

See it come down in the flood of centuries
to the tongue and throat,
like love, like a tornado, at times,
like a breast slashed by war
like a torn viscera.

See it come from the males
and females of the past
into the bloodstream of a creating,
inevitable magic.

How much memory of smile and grief!
Such fears amassed in its name!

And death's garden with its flowers
half-opened, opening, now open,
so the semen of cemeteries
will compose the blood of the sons.

If man would sail into blood
and know the sound of its anguish,
the gurgling of its instinct
and bubbling of its thought;
if man, like an eye inside blood
could see eternity and its minute
and the total edge of his destiny,
he would already know there is a single blood,
that of the dead and ours, burning.

Ardiendo desde ayer y para siempre
en cada voz,
en cada rayo
de la palabra y de la luz y el crimen.

Esta es la sangre nuestra.

Porque los dioses, los altivos dioses,
no tienen sangre.

Dejadla fluir
y que la boca de la herida cante.

Burning since yesterday and forever
in each voice,
in each ray
of the word, the light and the crime.

This is our own blood.

Because the gods, the haughty gods,
have no blood.

Let it flow
and let the mouth of the wound sing.

Selecciones de *Sólo la voz*

XXV

En la quinta estación,
la del olvido,
se detiene el coloquio de las sombras.

El invierno pasó,
muerto de frío.
Nadie se acuerda ya de su blancura.

Atrás, el tiempo se ha tendido,
muerto,
a no saber, a no soñar, a nada.

Y aquí están los viajeros.
Los de siempre:

—¿Quién eres tú?
¿De dónde?
¿Y a qué vienes?

Calla el viento en las copas de los árboles,
y nadie quiere responder.

Primero fue el otoño,
antes que el hielo.
Y en remolinos de oro
dejó caer sus pétalos.

—¿Quién eres, di, quién eres?

Y todavía ayer fue primavera.
Niños jugando sobre el ancho verde,
gritando contra el rostro de las flores.

—Pero dime, ¿quién eres?

Y anteayer,
el estío
lanza y fuego.
La panoja dorada, el sol ardido,
el amor en la palma de las manos,
la brasa cenital del mediodía.

Selections from *Sólo la voz*

XXV

In the fifth season,
the season of oblivion,
dialogues between the shadows cease.

Winter came to an end,
frozen to death.
No one recalls its whiteness anymore.

Behind us, time has stretched out,
dead,
from not knowing, not dreaming, from nothingness.

And here are the travelers.
The perennial ones:

—Who are you?
Where are you from?
Why have you come?

The wind hushes in the treetops;
no one is willing to answer.

First autumn came,
before the ice.
It dropped its petals
in golden whirlwinds.

—Who are you, tell me, who are you?

And only yesterday was spring.
Children playing in green expanses,
shouting into faces of flowers.

—But tell me, who are you?

And day before yesterday,
summer,
lance and fire,
Gilded cornsilk and sun inflamed,
love in the palms of our hands,
blazing zenith coal of midday.

—Te pregunto tu nombre
y el origen
de tus pies, de tu frente, de tus ojos.

Tiembla en el cielo oscuro,
arriba,
lejos,
una rosa de plata.

¿Mi nombre?
¿Tuve un nombre, acaso?
¿Y en qué tiempo?

En la más alta rama,
abre el buho tenaz su ojo de vidrio.

—I ask you your name
and the origin
of your face and eyes and feet.

Above and
far away,
a silver rose
quivers in the dark sky.

—My name?
Did I have a name, perhaps?
When was that?

On the highest branch,
the tenacious owl opens its glass eye.

XXXI

Hoy te dejas caer como una piedra al agua.
Como una frase viva
a la memoria,
como un largo estertor
cae entre las angustias de la alcoba.

Vienes con lo que fuiste.
Con tu sombra
pegada a la figura,
triste de andar contigo,
tu cosecha de espasmos,
tu vanidad,
tu honda
costumbre de esperar en la ventana
del tiempo, alguna rosa.

Vienes acompañado de tus gestos,
acariciando tu zozobra,
pastoreando las voces
congregadas en torno de tu boca.

¿De dónde a dónde caes?
¿Quién despeña
y en qué atmósfera,
lo que al formar tu imagen fue llenándola
de una fugaz historia?

¿Quién serás de hoy en más,
barro caído,
bandera arriada,
trayectoria muerta?

¿Quién, sino tu recuerdo,
la dimensión difusa del olvido,
la palabra entredicha a los albores,
y el rumor de tu sombra
deslizándose
por donde se deslizan otras sombras?

XXXI

Today you fall as a stone to water.
As a vivid phrase
falls to memory,
as a prolonged gasp
falls among agonies of a bedroom.

You come accompanied by all you were.
Your shadow
firm to your figure,
sad from joining you,
your harvest of spasms,
your vanity,
your deepened
custom of long waiting at the window
of time, for some rose.

Your gestures also accompany you,
caressing your anxiety,
shepherding voices
that are gathered about your mouth.

From where into where do you fall?
To what atmosphere,
who is scattering
all that formed and filled your image
with its elusive history?

Fallen clay,
lowered banner,
dead projectile,
after today who will you be?

Who other than your memory,
diffused dimension of oblivion,
word forbidden at dawn,
and sound of your shadow
slipping away
  along the path with other shadows?

Selecciones de *Este pequeño siempre*

En la memoria de la primavera

A los poetas venezolanos, en los nombres
fraternos de Otto de Sola y Vicente Gerbasi

Tomas las rosa,
dejas
caer en ella
la luz de las pupilas.
Enumeras los pétalos,
la detienes,
la giras,
conversas con la curva que se curva en la orilla,
y es otra rosa siempre,
a cada instante,
desde el aroma hasta la espina.

Mi tiempo,
mi circunstancia grata o dolorida,
tu estar,
tu estar ausente,
es también esta rosa
tuya,
mía.

Cada vez que le damos media vuelta
entre los dedos
a esta pequeña rosa de la vida,
le descubrimos un secreto nuevo
o una fragancia antigua.

La forma se repite
siempre varia,
siempre la misma.
En la memoria de la primavera
algo se llama rosa,
y se recuerda
cada vez que la luz se dulcifica.

Selections from *Este pequeño siempre*

In Memory of Spring

To the Venezuelan poets, through the fraternal names
of Otto de Sola and Vicente Gerbasi

You pick up the rose,
into it
you drop
light from the eyes.
You number the petals,
and hold it still,
and whirl it about,
and chat with the curve that curves around it,
and it's always another rose,
at every instant,
from its aroma to its thorn.

My time,
my pleasant or painful circumstance,
your presence,
your present absence,
is also this rose
yours,
mine.

Each time we turn it halfway
between our fingers—
this small rose of life—
we discover a new secret
or an old aroma.

The shape is similar
but always different,
always the same.
In memory of spring
something is called a rose,
and it's remembered
whenever the light softens.

Hoy hablo de la rosa
porque es imprescindible que ella exista.
Porque necesitamos afirmarla
y afirmarnos
en su delgada línea.

Ya venimos de vuelta del abrojo y el cardo,
ya transitamos la maleza
ya pasamos el patio de la ortiga.
Séanos permitido estar en gracia
de la rosa,
que es un modo de estar en gracia humana,
casi divina.

Se me dirá: "no es hora
de cantar a la rosa, *more antica.*"
No importa. Aún las abejas
liban.

También esto es verdad.
También estamos
en la mitad magnífica.
También el sol reclama su palabra,
la esperanza una voz que la bendiga.

Y todo forma parte del mismo tiempo nuestro,
del mismo que discurre o que desliza
bajo nuestro implacable testimonio
y el fervor que lo anima.

Es necesario que la rosa exista.
Que brote,
que ilumine,
que se extinga.
Que en el costado de la luz, su sangre
eterna y fugacísima,
nos deje pensativos y extasiados
y nos otorgue su lección de brisa.

I speak today about the rose
because it is not expendable,
because we must affirm it
and affirm ourselves
in its slender line.

Now we return from the thistle and the briar,
now we cross the brambles
now we pass the patio of the nettle.
Let it be granted to us to be in the grace
of the rose,
one way to be in human grace
but almost divine.

Some will tell me: "this is not the time
to sing of the rose, *more antica*."
It doesn't matter. Even the bees
find nourishment there.

This is also true.
We are also
within the marvellous half.
The sun also demands its word,
and hope, a voice to bless it.

And all is part of our same time,
the same time that scurries by and slips
under our inexorable witness
and the fervor that gives it life.

It's necessary for the rose to exist.
Let it bud,
let it shine brightly
and be extinguished.
Let the side of the light
with its very fleeting, eternal blood
leave us thoughtful and enthralled
and bestow upon us its lesson of breeze.

Adalid de la muerte

A Miguel Angel Asturias, y en él
a los poetas de Guatemala

Vengo a pedir la paz, fusil en mano,
a exigir el amor con bayonetas,
a mejorar el mundo con rayo, sangre y muerte,
a bendecir la historia con viudas y cadáveres.
Vengo a encender lámparas tenebrosas,
a acariciar cabellos bífidos de medusa,
a elevar en el asta más alta de este día
banderas de peligro, con franjas paralelas de rencor y de odio.

Soy así el redentor en un espejo negro.
El que arrebata el pan al miserable.
El que cercena a la doncella, el virgen,
el intacto milagro de los pechos.
Soy el arrasador de los anchos cultivos.
El que pronuncia largos discursos en la plaza,
y promete en el nombre del hombre lo que sabe
que no se cumplirá nunca en la tierra.

Soy el farsante, el que extorsiona, el que asesina,
y busca una palabra noble y sonora para apoyar su infamia.
El que en olor de amor y de servicio
derriba aviones,
hunde barcos,
destroza monumentos y edificios.

Vengo a parlamentar a dentelladas.
A esgrimir la razón del poderío.
"In gold we trust", en el estiércol rubio
y en el lodo podrido y en el rancio sudor de las dolientes
                                          multitudes.
Yo soy el que pronuncia horas enteras de justificaciones,
el que maneja rebaños de empecinadas esperanzas,
el que tuerce el sentido, la voluntad, la imagen
desde pantallas, televisores, radios y carteleras.

Death Commander

To Miguel Angel Asturias and through him
to the poets of Guatemala

I come asking for peace, rifle in hand,
demanding love, with bayonets,
to make the world better with lightning bolt, blood and death,
to bless History with widows and cadavers.
I come to light the lamps of darkness,
to stroke the split medusa-hair of the jellyfish,
today, from the tallest pole, to fly danger flags
with parallel borders of hatred and rancor.

Thus I am the redeemer in a black mirror.
Who snatches bread from the wretched,
who shears from the maiden the virgin
untouched miracle of her breasts.
I am the ravager of ample harvests,
who delivers long speeches in the plaza,
promising in the name of man what he knows
will never be fulfilled on earth.

I am the buffoon, who swindles and assassinates,
and seeks noble, sonorous words to support his infamy.
Who sporting airs of love and service
shoots down planes,
sinks ships,
destroys monuments and buildings.

I come to arbitrate, teeth bared.
To blandish the reasoning of the power structure,
"In gold we trust, in the blond manure,
rotten mud, and rancid sweat of suffering multitudes.

I am the one who hour after hour, proclaims justifications,
manipulates flocks of stubborn hopes,
projects deformed meanings, desires, and images
from movie screen, television, radio and poster.

Yo soy el inventor de una frase latina
que han de saberse de memoria todos los estudiantes:
"*Si vis pace, para bellum*", digo.
Y vendo municiones de distintos calibres,
pago barato el sol que tuesta los lomos campesinos,
o raciono el azúcar, la leche, la confianza entre hermanos

Soy el espía. El delator. El hijo que denuncia a su madre.
El ejemplo, el modelo, el paradigma, el camarada.
Soy el cabal artífice del destierro,
el juez que embriaga pueblos enteros en el circo romano,
el rectilíneo, insobornable, perfecto agente de la historia.

Ya estuve en otras partes y en otros tiempos. Vengo
desde el dolmen, pasando por mil tronos y truenos.
No me importa el color ni el dolor del hundido.
Toda doctrina es buena si sirve a mi designio.
Sólo he cambiado el modo, los instrumentos, nada
que me resulte sustancial. La honda,
la flecha,
la catapulta o el mosquete
ya están en el desván de los desechos inservibles.

Son mis grandes aliados los elementos más pequeños:
la ampolla de invisibles bacterias
que invade una región sin que un oído escuche su solapada marcha,
el pedazo de un átomo roto en millares de fragmentos heroicos,
el burócrata frío, anodino, puesto por mí entre el hambre y la rutina
el sueño lento, suave, deleitable del opio,
las alucinaciones de la dietilamida del ácido lisérgico,
la reducción metódica
científica,
en los precios menguados de las materias primas.
Soy el Gerente General de los maricones y las putas.
Soy la mitad de abajo del sello salomónico.
Soy el espejo de mercurio.

I am the inventor of the Latin expression
that all students must memorize:
"*Si vis pace, para bellum,*" I say.
And I sell munitions of different calibre:
I pay cheaply for the sun that toasts laborers' backs,
or I ration the sugar, the milk, and trust between brothers.

I am the spy. The informer. The son who denounces his mother.
The example, the model, the paradigm, the comrade.
I am the expert author of exiles,
the judge who inebriates an entire populace in a Roman circus,
the upright, unimpeachable, perfect representative of History.

I have already been in other places and other times.
Since the Dolmen, I have traversed a thousand thunders and thrones.
The color or grief of the drowned is not my concern.
Any doctrine suffices that serves my ends.
I have only changed the manner, the tools, nothing
of substance. The slingshot,
the arrow,
the catapult or the musket
are now in the attic with the useless rubbish.

My great allies are the smallest items:
the ampule of invisible bacteria
that invades without any ear's sensing its insidious march,
the fragment of a shattered atom of thousands of heroic pieces,
the cold, ineffectual bureaucrat set by me between routine and hunger,
the slow, delectable, soothing opium dream,
the hallucinations of lisergic diethylamide,
the scientific,
methodical reduction
of the diminishing prices of raw materials.
I am the General Manager of prostitutes and fairies,
I am the bottom half of the sarsaparilla.
I am the mercury mirror.

Vengo a pedir la paz para meterla
en este saco de granadas,
a exigir el amor para arrimarlo al napalm,
a decir mi discurso patriótico y solemne
mientras mis carpinteros elevan la gran tarima del cadalso.

Un día
mis ojos han de ver toda esta tierra devastada.
Hecha vidrio la arena del desierto,
secas al sol las algas submarinas.
Diré talvez, repitiendo mis propias y viejas locuciones
"Delenda est Cartago"
"Here was Granada"
Lídice
My Lai
La primavera de Praga
Siberia.
El "apartheid" o Belfast.

Y seguiré mi rumbo pacifista y magnánimo,
rico de sabotajes, de plagios, de secuestros,
hasta aprender un día, si aprendo, si comprendo,
que el odio multiplica sus pólenes de odio,
y que no habrá descanso
mientras yo mismo, el hombre,
busque por derroteros de violencia y mentira
la redención del hombre que soy, que eres, que somos.

I come asking for peace to put it
in this sack of granades,
demanding love to put it with the napalm.
to deliver my solemn, patriotic speech
while my carpenters raise the great platform of the gallows.

One day
my eyes will see the devastation of this land.
The desert sand turned to glass,
the sea algae dried in the sun.
Perhaps I will say, repeating my own old speeches
"Delenda est Cartago"
"Here was Granada"
Lidice
My Lai
Springtime in Prague
Siberia
Apartheid or Belfast.

And I will continue my magnanimous pacifistic path,
with its wealth of sabotage, plagiarism, kidnappings,
until I learn one day, if I do, if I do understand,
that hatred multiplies its pollen of hate,
and that there will be no rest
while I myself, man,
search along paths of violence and falsehood
for redemption for the man that I, that you, that we are.

Selecciones de *Fácil palabra*

1

Fácil sería la palabra
sin hojas.
Fácil como un vacío.
Como una sombra.
Pero ocurre al contrario: te arrimas al silencio
y ella te acosa
llena de ideas,
de memorias,
siempre con algo entre las manos.
Y simplemente no la logras
desnuda,
sola.

2

Palabra que persigues
y no es palabra.
Si la encuentras, encuentras
sólo una cáscara.

8

Fácil palabra, digo.
Y aprendo, repitiéndolo, que es vano
buscarla. La pretendo como un aire que cruza,
pero rica de espacio.

10

Divaguemos mejor.
Digamos algo
tan insignificante, que ni el eco
se dé por enterado.

Selections from *Fácil palabra*

1

Easy would the word be
if it did not sprout leaves.
Easy like an empty space.
Like a shadow.
But the opposite occurs: you approach silence
and it assaults you
filled with ideas,
with memories,
always handling something,
and you simply do not attain it
naked,
alone.

2

A word you pursue
and it is not the word.
If you do find one, you find
only a shell.

8

An easy word, I say.
And I learn, by repeating it, that in vain
is it sought. I intend it as a passing breeze,
but rich in space.

10

Let us digress further.
Let us say something
so insignificant, that even the echo
will pretend not to know.

16

Me parece que estoy apuntando minucias.
Creando un lenguaje de impalpable arena.
Dibujando en el aire la curva que se escapa,
y el gesto que se queda.
Y es muy posible que esto carezca de importancia.
O que la tenga.

33

Fácil palabra. Nunca hubo palabra
fácil para entregar ni recibirse.
Siempre el trayecto le cortó las alas,
el aire avaro le robó matices
y ese fervor con que la pronunciamos
redujo la fragancia de su origen.
Aprende en ello que si amor te digo
es más amor de lo que tú percibes:
que te llega el reflejo y eso basta
para que te circunde y te ilumine.

41

Hace un silencio estaba
pendiente del murmullo.
"Talvez cae—me dije—la palabra sin hojas."
Cayó sin fruto.

43

Pero digo una rosa:
tú entiendes otra.
Pero digo una herida:
pienso en la mía.
Pero digo un recuerdo:
no está en tu tiempo.
Y si el amor te digo,
¿sientes el mismo?

16

I seem to be jotting down trifles.
Creating a language of intangible sand.
Drawing in the air the curve that is escaping,
and the suggestion of it that remains.
And very possibly this isn't important.
Or it is.

33*

An easy word. There was never a word
easy to deliver nor to receive.
For the journey has always clipped its wings,
greedy air stolen its shades of meaning,
and, in saying it, our very fervor
diminished the fragrance of its source.
Be aware when I say the word love
the love is greater than you imagine:
the mirror image you receive is enough
to embrace you and enlighten you.

41

A silence ago, I was
listening for the sound.
"Perhaps it will fall—I said to myself—
the word without leaves." It fell without fruit.

43

But I speak of a rose:
you understand another.
But I speak of a wound:
I think of my own.
But I speak of a memory:
it's not from your time.
And if love is what I say,
is it the love you feel?

*No. 33 was first published in *La estafeta*, Madrid, 1971,
as number 32.

78

Abreme, luz, la ventana.
Ventana, ábreme la luz.

79

El paisaje, la atmósfera, la vida,
no están aquí ni allá.
Los hallarás, si con amor los buscas,
en lo que fue, lo que es, lo que será.
Que el alma vive atada al tiempo firme,
no al espacio fugaz.

88

Yo vengo de mi palabra
y hacia mi palabra voy,
que en el principio era el Verbo
y yo, su persecución.

107

¿El Rey de Oros? ¡Alto!
Es mío el juego, porque
se ha posado en mi mano
el As de Ruiseñores.

160

Un pájaro feo
grazna
y otea desde el alféizar
de mi ventana.
Hallo su crítica
falso:
si él supiera de poesía,
trinaría, y no graznara.

78

Open the window for me, light.
Window, open the light for me.

79

Life, the atmosphere, the landscape
are neither here nor there.
You'll find them if you ardently search for them
in what used to be, what is, and what is yet to come.
For the soul is tied to a firm time,
not to a fleeting space.

88

I come from my word
and toward my word I go,
for in the beginning was the Word
and I, its pursuit.

107

The King of Diamonds? Stop!
The play is mine; you see
what landed in my hand—
the Ace of Nightingales.

160

An ugly bird
squawks
and ogles from my window
sill.
I find his criticism
false:
if he knew about poetry,
he would sing and not squawk.

En un cuento para niños
hay una rana, un estanque,
un príncipe, y una magia
cuyo origen no se sabe.
Cuando al fin lo comprendemos,
ya es muy tarde.

El viento trae de los pinos
una ancha música,
una ancha música aromada,
verde, que ondula
por los cinco sentidos
limpia y desnuda.

170

In a children's story
there's a frog, a pool,
a prince, and a magic
of unknown origin.
When we finally understand,
it's already too late.

195

The wind brings from the pines
a full music,
a full, aromatic
green music, that undulates
through the five senses
pure and bare.

Selecciones de *Prólogo a la noche*

El gris perfecto

¡Oh, gris, hijo del gris, en quien reposa
la sucesión de grises invariables!
Como en la playa inmensa, en tí recalan
hechos gris, los colores de la tarde.
Y más allá de ti
nada asciende ni cae,
porque la luz que te encontró, se aduerme
en tu pradera gris de austeridades.

Vienes de la fogata
sabia en danza de rojos infernales,
de soterraños índigos
y amarillos vibrantes.

Ya sufriste el oficio
de las llamas fugaces
y la tortura que retuerce el humo
en dolorosas voluptuosidades.

Ya supiste el chasquido en que besabas
los invisibles párpados del aire
y el júbilo de estar sobre la tierra
junto al susurro verde de los árboles.

Hoy, de vuelta,
has detenido el viaje,
y gris, gris de cabello, de ceniza,
nadie podrá encenderte ni apagarte.

San Salvador,
septiembre, 1981.

144

Selections from *Prólogo a la noche*

The Perfect Grey

Oh, grey, son of grey, in whom repose
the succession of invariable greys!
The now greyed colors of the afternoon
beat against you as against the immense shore.
And beyond you
nothing is rising or falling,
for the light that discovered you, drowses
in your grey meadow of austerities.

You come from the bonfire
wise in the dance of infernal reds,
subterranean indigos
and vibrant yellows.

You have already endured the workings
of the swirling flames,
the torture that twists the smoke
into sorrowful seductions.

You have already known the smacking sound
when you kissed the air's invisible eyelids
and the joy of being upon earth
near the green whispers of the trees.

In returning today,
you have stopped the journey
and grey, grey of hair and of ashes,
no one can now set you aflame or smother your fire.

San Salvador,
Sept., 1981.

Seis versos

—¿Por qué si hay tanta amargura
hablas de la flor y el beso,
la armonía y la ternura?
¿Por qué si hay tanta amargura
persistes en tu locura?

—Precisamente por eso.

San Salvador,
nov., 1982.

Six Lines

—Why when there is so much bitterness
do you speak of the flower and the kiss
harmony and bliss?
Why when there is so much bitterness
do you in your madness persist?

—Precisely, because of this.

San Salvador,
Nov., 1982.

Selección de *Casi en la luz*

Entre palabras

A Elizabeth Miller, la excelente
traductora de *Sólo la voz*, y dilecta
amiga de

Yo anduve entre palabras.
Amaba sus perfiles, tornadizos o estáticos,
su doble ser de sílaba y secreto,
la agudeza de las letras con filo
penetrando como agrios fermentos en el alma.

Era aquello ir andando
entre la madurez de ocultas músicas
y descubriendo en ellas
signos apenas, gestos, menudas reverencias
a una verdad que huía.

No era una vanidad de oídos puros
prestos a la cadencia, al ritmo, al canto,
sino algo más:
un sacramento: un lúcido
sentir la creación por la palabra,
hacer surgir los seres desde la entraña de las voces
y anticipar sus luchas todavía en proyecto.

De la queja al dolor, ¿qué espacio queda?
¿Por qué no recorrer esta distancia
yendo ahora del grito a la tortura,
o del beso al amor,
o del sudario
a la concreta imagen del reposo?

Selection from *Casi en la luz*

Between Words

To Elizabeth Miller, the fine
translator of *Sólo la voz* and
dear friend of Hugo Lindo

I travelled between words.
I loved their shapes, shifting or motionless,
their double essence of meaning and mystery,
the incisiveness of sharp-edged letters
like sour ferments infiltrating the soul.

I was traveling the full resonance
of hidden harmonies
to discover within their music
minute signs and gestures, gentle nods
honoring elusive truths.

Not merely a display of sounds
for rhythm, cadence or song,
but something more:
a rite of devotion: lucid sensitivity
to create through the word,
to draw living entities from its innermost recesses,
to anticipate its inevitable struggles.

What distance lies between moan and pain?
Why not span this interval,
move from scream to torture,
and from kiss to love,
or from shroud
to the solid figure in repose?

Cuando hablo soy el mago en el conjuro,
el tiempo acumulando verdes en la semilla,
soy la semilla misma
o el inicio del viento casi brisa en la aldea,
que agitará más tarde sus aspas de catástrofe.
O el orgasmo,
el recio, el crudo orgasmo generador de sombras
y pastor de la historia y de la sangre.

La palabra es mi oficio y sacrificio.
Es la prisión sonora y sin murallas
donde la libertad halla acomodo:
lo demás surge de ella.
        Todo el mundo se allana
a su secreta realidad,
al tono y al acento,
a los contornos
de su tañido,
a la sustancia música,
a la escultura vaga de sus formas.

Pero llega el instante
de construir la palabra con silencios,
con reticencias largas, con memorias
que no se dicen, con fantasmas
entrevistas apenas en la leche del sueño.

Y uno se halla de nuevo a la orilla del mar.
Con un cansancio tierno en la bahía gris de las retinas,
dibujando en el aire
cosas que no se ven,
cantando cosas que tampoco se escuchan,
pero transido
de una redonda plenitud
que es casi dolorosa.

San Salvador,
noviembre de 1981

I speak and I am the magician casting his spell,
the greening time within the seed.
I am the seed itself
or rising wind, a soft breeze in the village,
which later will flail its wings of catastrophe.
Or I am the orgasm,
the strong, the harsh orgasm, creator of shadows,
pastor of history and of blood.

Within the word lies my duty and my destruction.
From this echoing prison without walls
where freedom fashions its place
all else emerges.
    All creation is contoured
to its secret reality,
its tone and accent,
the shape
of its chord,
its musical inclination,
the vague configuration of its forms.

And the moment comes
to construe the word with silences,
with lingering insinuations, with memories
unspoken, and apparitions
scarcely glimpsed in the milky haze of dreams.

Again one faces the water's edge.
With sensitive weariness in the retinas' gray deeps,
sketching in the air
things unseen,
singing of things unheard
and overwhelmed
by replete wholeness
that is near to pain.

San Salvador,
November, 1981

Hugo Lindo: *In Memoriam*

por David Escobar Galindo

La poesía de Hugo Lindo (1917-1985) es, en El Salvador, un hito fundamental, tanto para comprender el desarrollo global del pensamiento lírico nacional cuanto para dar muestra de una de las características más salientes del espíritu salvadoreño: el ansia de universalidad, que pugna por superar la pequeñez geográfica y la marginalidad histórica del país.

Surge Hugo Lindo, con una poesía formalmente madura y conceptualmente cargada de inquietudes metafísicas, a mediados de la década de los cuarentas—aunque su labor juvenil remonta a muchos años antes—, en el momento también en que las Democracias aliadas están por vencer a las potencias del Eje en la Segunda Guerra Mundial. Es un instante histórico de convulsión y de esperanzas, que da a los creadores—sólo en ese instante, porque luego, con el inicio inmediato de la "guerra fría" el mundo se dio cuenta de que la Guerra había sido un trágico juego de equívocos—una renovada fe en la conciencia del hombre y en la palabra que la hace comunicable.

Hugo Lindo—joven inteligente, audaz, ansioso de gloria y muy bien dotado para el vuelo filosófico—plasma su visión de ese tiempo en poemas grandiosos como "Las cuatro dimensiones del instante", de 1942; y, por otra parte, dando muestras de un anhelo religioso que por entonces se orientaba hacia un catolicismo ortodoxo y luego lo haría hacia una progresiva interiorización en las más elevadas doctrinas de la religiosidad oriental, deja testimonio de sus éstasis de hombre de fe en su *Poema eucarístico*, también de 1942, que es una verdadera joya de expresión lírica depurada y de intensa concentración espiritual.

A partir de ese momento, Hugo Lindo parece tomar plena posesión de su destino de poeta, y se lanza—guarnecido con todos los recursos de una amplia cultura humanística—a las aventuras mayores del hombre que piensa y que sueña, integrando en uno ambos ejercicios espirituales. La primera estación se llama *Libro de horas*, de 1947, en la que el poeta toma posesión de la tragedia personal del tiempo, que ciñe al hombre a fronteras definidas; y el segundo momento tiene por nombre *Sinfonía del límite*, rapsodia cósmica en que el tiempo individual se confronta con el espacio supraindividual, en una tensión de contrarios que se aman y se repelen a la vez, dando origen y significado al drama vivo y perpetuo de la historia. Es el hombre que lleva un reloj en las entrañas, a quien cada golpe del minutero le recuerda la limitación de su poder y, al mismo tiempo, por tremenda paradoja, el desafío insoslayable de su sed de eternidad.

Hugo Lindo: *In Memoriam*

by David Escobar Galindo

The poetry of Hugo Lindo (1917-1985) is an essential benchmark in the development of El Salvador's lyrical thought toward global dimensions. His poetry exemplifies the Salvadoran spirit in its attempt to overcome geographic smallness and historical marginality and reach the universal. The poetic voice of Hugo Lindo came into prominence in the forties, its youthful expression refined and charged with metaphysical disquietude. The Salvadoran dictatorship of General Hernández was in collapse and the Allies were on the verge of defeating the Axis powers in World War II. This historic moment of immense excitement and hope preceded the imminent recognition of the war as a tragic, fallacious exercise. But in those first moments before the "Cold War" writers experienced a renewed faith in the conscience of man and in the word to communicate it.

Hugo Lindo was bright, eager and enterprising, and he was well equipped for traveling philosophical paths. He expressed his vision of that time in grandiloquent poems like "Las cuatro dimensiones del instante" (The Four Dimensions of the Moment), 1942. He also gave voice to his religious zeal, then of an orthodox catholic orientation, which later moved progressively toward introspection inspired by Eastern religious doctrine. His zeal as a man of faith found expression in his "*Poema eucarístico*" (Eucharist Poem), also of 1942. This poem is a veritable jewel of intense spiritual density and pure lyricism.

With his future as a poet now assured, and with a broad humanistic education in hand, Hugo Lindo ventured forth as a thinker and a dreamer, these spiritual exercises fusing into one. His first stop along the journey was *Libro de horas* (Book of Hours), 1947, a volume in which the poet possesses Time's tragic fate which binds man to defined boundaries. His second destination, entitled *Sinfonía del límite* (Symphony of Limits), is a cosmic rhapsody in which individual time/space confronts supra-individual space in a tension of opposites. The constant attraction and rejection is the substance of the perpetual, historical drama. Man's inner clock and each of the minute-hand's movements remind him of the limits of his power while, paradoxically, he is simultaneously and equally threatened by his inevitable thirst for eternity.

Nadie antes, en la poesía salvadoreña, había tocado tan imperiosamente a la puerta del misterio ontológico como lo hace Hugo Lindo. Eso abre un boquete luminoso en nuestra cultura, por el que han de colarse otras voces, igualmente anhelosas de vuelos trascendentales. A partir de *Sinfonía del límite*, publicada en 1953 pero escrita en 1949, el poeta parece tener muchos momentos de natural vacilación. El empeño ha sido tan atrevido, tan original y tan logrado, que el poeta— quizás inconscientemente—busca, durante años, otras rutas expresivas. Sesga hacia la novela, con ímpetu vigoroso, con decidida voluntad creadora; pero su capacidad narrativa no alcanza las alturas de su inspiración poética, y, aunque en 1956 había publicado en el número 10 de la revista *Cultura*, de San Salvador, un "Testamento lírico", en el que voluntariamente da por concluida su carrera lírica, vuelve al poema orgánico en 1962, con su caudaloso *Navegante río*, que retoma los hilos de su reto a los misteriosos poderíos de la palabra, y lo hace lanzando esos hilos fulgurantes sobre la marea convulsa del tiempo histórico. El hombre maduro que es por entonces Hugo Lindo plasma en ese libro mayor la temperatura de su destino, que reverbera en llamas de telúrico holocausto. Al hombre que piensa y sueña se une aquí—en trinidad de fortaleza viril— el hombre que sufre en el "aquí" y en el "ahora".

De ahí, del *Navegante río*, surge luego el delta de brazos complementarios, íntimos y colectivos: *Sólo la voz, Maneras de llover, Este pequeño siempre*.... Pero todo río—y de eso no escapa el río iluminado de la sangre—llega al mar. Lo sabíamos de toda la vida, pero Manrique nos lo dijo tan sabiamente que, a partir de él, todos los océanos son el océano del morir. Hacia ese océano inexorable y deseado se dirige, pues, el río navegante. Y, en el caso de Hugo Lindo, tal océano es atalayado, atisbado, sentido con palpitante conciencia cotidiana en sus últimos años, dolorosos de enfermedad pero rutilantes de espera fecunda. Sus últimos libros están llenos de luz, porque son, como reza el título de uno de ellos, el *Prólogo a la noche*. El poeta regresa, confiado y entero, a los brazos de una divinidad que no conoce, pero que le es tan familiar como su propio cuerpo, como su misma sangre, como su total indefensión invencible.

La obra de Hugo Lindo es un ciclo perfecto. El poeta estuvo siempre obsesionado por las categorías racionales, y la razón—fiel e implacable—le dio a su vida la forma de una sinfonía. A la hora postrera, el legado del poeta es, sin embargo, una nota abierta, inesperada y transparente, que se le escapa a la razón: la nota que repite un eco, el eco que repite la inefable nostalgia del misterio. Es decir: todo queda abierto—preguntas, sueños, agonías—para que otros ensayen, sin fin, la religiosidad audaz de la poesía que no muere. Así sea.

San Salvador, abril, 1986.

No one before, in Salvadoran poetry, had knocked so imperiously at the door of ontological mystery as Hugo Lindo. Thus he opened a small, bright space that attracted other voices desirous of transcendental excursions. After *Sinfonía del límite*, 1949, published in 1953, the poet had moments of hesitation. He had been so daring, so original and so successful, that for years he searched, perhaps unconsciously, for other expressive modes. With vigorous and creative determination he diverted his attention to the novel. His narratives, however, did not reach the heights of his poetic inspiration. In 1956, number ten of the journal *Cultura* of San Salvador published his *Testamento lírico* (Lyrical Declaration) in which he gave up his career as a poet. But he returned to the organic poem in 1962. With his mighty *Navegante río* (Sailing River) he picked up the threads of his challenge to the mysterious powers of the word. He did so by casting those resplendent threads over the turbulent tide of historic time. The burning intensity of his later works is evident in this major book that glows in flames of a telluric holocaust. To the thinker and the dreamer is joined—in a trinity of virile strength—the man who suffers in the "here" and "now."

From *Navegante río* emerged the delta of intimate and collective branches: *Sólo la voz, Maneras de llover, Este pequeño siempre...(Only the Voice, The Ways of Rain, This Little Bit of Always)*. Each river—even that of the blood—reaches the sea. Though it might be self-evident, since Manrique,[1] every ocean has become for us the ocean of death. Toward that inexorable, desired ocean the *río navegante* (river sailor) made his way. And, in Hugo Lindo's case, the ocean was surveyed, observed and fervently felt. In his later years he suffered from illness, but he was sustained by a vibrant, productive hope. His last books are filled with light, because, as the title of one of them betrays, they are the *Prólogo a la noche* (Prologue to Night). Feeling confident and whole, the poet has returned to the arms of a divinity he hasn't met, yet who is as familiar to him as his own body and blood, as his complete invincible defenselessness.

The works of Hugo Lindo turn a full cycle. The poet was always concerned with categories and rational thinking. Faithful, implacable logic gave his life a symphonic form. Nevertheless, his final legacy is an open note—unpredicted, transparent, eluding reason: a note that echoes, the echo of the ineffable nostalgia for mystery. Everything—questions, dreams, miseries—is without resolution so that others will attempt the daring religious endeavor toward poetry that does not die. May it be so.

[1]Jorge Manrique, (1440?-1479). In*"Coplas por la muerte de su padre"*: "Nuestras vidas son los ríos/ que van a dar en la mar/ que es el morir:" (Our lives are the rivers that reach the sea/ that is death.)

Biographical Sketch

Hugo Lindo, born October 13, 1917 in La Unión, El Salvador, died September 9, 1985, in San Salvador, leaving a wife, seven children and four granddaughters. He had served his nation as Minister of Education in 1961 and was Director Emeritus of the *Academia Salvadoreña de la Lengua*; a Corresponding Member of the Academies of Language of Honduras, Colombia, Chile and Spain; Director Emeritus for the Organization for Cultural Affairs of the Central American Countries (ODECA); and Ambassador Emeritus to Chile, Colombia, Spain and Egypt. Hugo Lindo was one of El Salvador's most distinguished authors, having received numerous prizes for his poetry, novels and short stories. His most recent literary honors include nomination for the Miguel Cervantes Prize of Spain by the *Academia Salvadoreña de la Lengua*, September, 1984, and an *Homenaje* by the *Academia Salvadoreña*, the *Ateneo de El Salvador* and the *Instituto Sanmartiniano Salvadoreño*, November 18, 1984.

Photograph, November 16, 1984 (EGM)

Bibliography

Poetry

Fácil palabra. Colección Hugo Lindo Poesía, vol. 2, San Salvador: Editorial Todos Uno, 1985; *Resonancia de Vivaldi.* San Salvador: Flores-Alvarenga Editores, 1976; *Sangre de Hispania fecunda.* San Salvador: Ministerio de Educación, 1972; *Este pequeño siempre.* León, España: Colección Provincia, 1971; *Maneras de llover.* Madrid: Ediciones Cultura Hispánica, 1968; 2nd ed. San Salvador: Ministerio de Educación, 1982; *Sólo la voz.* San Salvador: Ministerio de Educación, 1967, incl. in *Hugo Lindo: Sólo la voz/ Only the Voice.* Richardson, TX: Mundus Artium Press, 1984; *Navegante río.* San Salvador: Ministerio de Educación, 1963; *Varia poesía.* (a reprint collection) San Salvador: Ministerio de Educación, 1961; *Trece instantes.* Montevideo, Uruguay: Cuadernos Julio Herrera y Reissig, 1959; incl. in *Varia poesía; Sinfonía del límite.* San Salvador: Direc. Gnrl. de Bellas Artes, 1953, incl. in *Varia poesía; Libro de horas.* Guatemala: Editorial "El Libro de Guatemala," México: Talleres de Editorial "B. Costa-Amic," 1948; 2nd ed. San Salvador: Biblioteca Universitaria, vol. XIX, Talleres de Editorial Ahora, 1950; *Poema eucarístico y otros.* San Salvador: Talleres Gráficos Cisneros, 1943, included in *Varia poesía,* 1961.

Reviews of Maneras de llover

César Aller, *Poesía española,* no. 207, Madrid, marzo, 1970; Estela Castelao, *Foro literario,* Uruguay, agosto, 1983; Oscar Echeverri Mejía, "Occidente," Cali, Colombia, 7 enero, 1983; Sonya Ingwersen, *Chasqui,* Ariz. St. U, 1986, "La prensa gráfica," San Salvador, 1984; Italo López Vallecillos, *Estudios centroamericanos,* San Salvador, dic., 1982: 93-96; H. Montes, "La tercera," Santiago de Chile, 28 nov., 1982; reprint. San Salvador, "Diario de Hoy," 15 enero, 1983; Joseph Vélez, "Ovaciones," México, 8 febrero, 1983.

Literary Prizes: Poetry

Sólo la voz, 2nd prize, Certamen nacional, El Salvador, 1967.
Navegante río, 1st prize, Quetzaltenango, Guatemala, 1962.
Libro de horas, 1st prize, "15 de septiembre," Guatemala, 1947.
Figura y alabanza de don Miguel de Cervantes Saavedra, "Cervantes, Sociedad de Beneficencia Española," 1946.
Preces a nuestra Sra. de la Paz, 2nd prize, San Miguel, 1943.
Trilogía de la ternura, gold medal, Santa Ana, 1935.

Novels

Yo soy la memoria. San Salvador: UCA/ Editores, 1983; *Cada día tiene su afán.* San Salvador: Ministerio de Educación, 1965; *¡Justicia Sr. Gobernador!* San Salvador: Ministerio de Educación, 1960; 4th ed., San Salvador: Ministerio de Educación, 1977; *El anzuelo de Dios.* Santiago, Chile: Editorial Zig Zag, 1956; reprint ed., San Salvador: Ministerio de Educación, 1963.

Short Stories

Guaro y champaña. San Salvador: By the Author, 1947; 3rd. ed. Ministerio de Educación, 1961; *Aquí se cuentan cuentos.* Bogotá, Colombia: Editora Continente, 1960; reprint ed., Ministerio de Educación, 1978; *Espejos paralelos.* San José, Costa Rica: Educa, 1974.

Essays

Recuento (Anotaciones literarias e históricas de Centro-américa). Colección Contemporáneos. San Salvador: Ministerio de Educación, 1969.

San Salvador, 8 Sept. 1983.

Pro'.
Elizabeth Miller,
South Methodist University,
Dalla, Tex.

Mi estimada amiga:

El correo de ayer me trajo su excelente
estudio sobre Maneras de Llover, con una traducción, que
me parece muy bien lograda, de varios cantos del libro, y
de todo el Invierno de la Raza.

Estas líneas son sólo para acusarle recibo
y expresarle gratitud.

Sin embargo, aprovecho para contarle que
ya estoy corrigiendo pruebas de imprenta de mi novela Yo soy
la Memoria, que Ud. conoce. Se editará en un tipo de letra
muy claro y espaciado, y aparecerá, se me indica, hacia no-
viembre o diciembre. En mi trabajo de corrector, voy ya más
adelante de la mitad.

Preparo -dentro de mis actividades universi-
tarias- un par de conferencias sobre la Estética y la Litera-
tura en José Ortega y Gasset, cuyo centenario natal se cele-
bra este año. Espero que me queden bien, pues les estoy dando
mucha atención y esmero. Ya le mandaré copias, cuando llegue
el momento. No sé si podrían tener cabida allá, en alguna pu-
blicación, en español o en inglés. Ya se verá. No hay prisa
alguna.

Queda, como siempre, a sus pies,

TRANSLATOR'S BIOGRAPHICAL NOTE

Elizabeth Gamble Miller is Associate Professor of Foreign Languages and Literatures at Southern Methodist University, Dallas, where she teaches Spanish American Poetry and Translation Theory and Practice. She has a Ph. D. in Humanities from the University of Texas at Dallas; her dissertation is on the translation process. Her other published book-length translations include *Hugo Lindo Sólo la voz/ Only the Voice*, Mundus Artium Press, 1984, and *Fábulas/ Fables*, in collaboration with Helen D. Clement, David Escobar Galindo, Editorial Delgado, 1985. Her essay on the poetry of Hugo Lindo: "La inquietud del proceso creador hacia la palabra," in a translation by Josefina Barrera de García, was published in *Cultura*, 72, 1985: 55-71. She is editor of *ALTA Newsletter* of the American Literary Translators Association and is on the international editorial board of *Translation Review*. She was elected an *Académica Correspondiente* of the *Academia Salvadoreña de la Lengua* in April of 1985.